FINDING
MY WAY

FINDING MY WAY

Stories From The Adirondacks

JOHN W. DEAN

SEL PUBLICATIONS
Syracuse, New York

Published by Sel Publications, 3895 Howlett Hill Road, Syracuse, NY 13215
Printed in the United States

ISBN #978-0-578-79675-8

Acknowledgements

The effort it took to write this book was, to borrow the cliché, "a labor of love," since it brought back many fond memories of people and places.

There are several folks who helped make this book possible. The person most helpful and impactful was my stepfather, Bob Bayle, who, being a career educator and author of several books, took the time to not only edit my work, but to make suggestions of removing or adding material. My mother, Carol Bayle, who, in proofreading every chapter, often learned about my escapades for the first time. My stepsister, Jackie Gordon; Tim Bennett and Dave Danglis who took the time to 'edit the editor' to whom both Bob and I are thankful.

Next In line is my Uncle Allan who is included in much of my writing. I still believe that Uncle Allan, being a "man's man," loving football, skiing, boating and family (maybe not in that order) wanted a son so bad, after having four daughters, that he did everything with me that a dad would do with his son. For that I will always be grateful. I have to thank my Aunt Judy, Uncle Dave, Aunt Ginny and Uncle Bruce for their "recollection" of events. They were in their thirties when most of these events took place. I chuckle when I consider that I now join them in their 'senior citizen' status. Time flies.

There are certain individuals mentioned in the book that may or may not know the impact they had in my life simply by participating in an event with me. To those folks, I thank you.

Most importantly, I thank my family for partaking in the hikes, canoe trips and camping trips in which they may have felt forced to join on occasion. And lastly, I am thankful for my wife, Terri, and our six children who have been a great source of joy (and tribulation on hikes) about whom I certainly enjoy writing.

Uncle Allan, Aunt Joan, Coco and Terri
on the Raquette River

Contents

Introduction | 1

Kayak Adventures | 5

Black Bears | 17

Winter Camping | 23

Ice Hockey | 35

The Summer of 1973 | 45

Boy Scouts | 51

Slippery Slopes | 63

Lake George | 73

Laundromats | 85

Santanoni | 91

Baby Diver | 99

Prospect Mountain | 105

One Last Adventure | 111

Conclusion | 113

Introduction

Our annual family vacation began on Sunday, August 10, 2003. After driving several hours in a pouring rain, we pulled into the muddy gravel driveway of the camp we had rented on Chateaugay Lake, located on the northern tip of the Adirondack Park. I had found the camp for rent while driving to Plattsburgh for a meeting. Two teenagers, Jacob and Ryan; two twelve-year-olds, Danielle and her friend Emily; nine-year-old Shane; Grandpa Bill; Terri and myself arrived at the ranch-style camp in two cars and a utility trailer loaded with two canoes and sports equipment.

We often rented a camp for a week in mid-summer, randomly choosing locations throughout the Adirondacks until we eventually purchased our own camp. The camp at Chateaugay Lake, although not the fanciest of camps, was perfect for our blended group. It had three bedrooms, an attached bunk house right on the lake, a sprawling dock, a large yard, and plenty of privacy. Grandpa and the boys were overjoyed to sleep in the bunkhouse since they were "night owls" and the girls each grabbed a bedroom, which left the only unclaimed bedroom for Terri and me. We usually had the last pick on rooms on family trips.

The excitement of staying at the camp and renting a pontoon boat for the week fended off any initial discouragement from the low-hanging clouds and constant patter of rain on the roof and the dock. We unpacked our vehicles and trailer under the constant drips of rain off the overhanging leaves. After a quick dinner and a pot of coffee, Grandpa and the girls started playing Rummy. The three boys found a game of Risk on the camp bookcase and set up the board for a game. I was content to read one of the Adirondack magazines left, appropriately, next to the well-worn sofa in the living room.

Monday morning, we woke up to a steady downpour accompanied by thunder and lightning. As we made quick work of the product from the coffee maker, the boys picked up where they left off on their marathon Risk game. The girls and Grandpa Bill started bickering over the "official" Rummy rules before eventually dealing the cards. I found my comfortable spot on the inviting sofa next to the large picture window, now clouded over with condensation and with a sound of the pelting rain. Convenient to me, the property owner had left numerous books about the Adirondacks in the rustic bookcase that was water-stained from sitting under the window. We occupied our spaces throughout the day taking snack breaks and cat naps until one of the kids said, "I'm going for a walk in the rain." I was deep into a book and passed on the muddy trek down the road.

On our third day at the camp, the sun broke through and we all rushed out into the fresh air as if we'd been confined for months. After three days of moving the Risk game from floor to table and back with no winner, the boys dumped their game pieces into the box and put on their swimsuits. Grandpa, who was usually agreeable to anything, said, "I've had enough of this crap," and bolted to the dock. He had been wearing his swimsuit for the entire time it was raining. The remainder of the week we engaged in every lake activity we could think of, fully utilizing the pontoon boat.

On Thursday evening we went into Malone to pick up some groceries, only to find all the stores dark and without power. The Northeast power outage of 2003 was in full swing. When we were informed that the entire Northeast was blacked out, we thought it was odd that we still had power at our camp. When we returned to camp, the lights, refrigerator, and television were working fine and there certainly wasn't an emergency generator on the property. We assumed that the town of Chateaugay must have had its own power source but the bait shop down the lake had none. We never knew why we were spared, but we were grateful. I was able to continue reading about the Adirondacks and the Rummy games could go on into the night.

By the time the week was over I had read two books, numerous magazines and shared several stories with my family of my Adirondack experiences as a youth. I noticed that wherever we rented a camp there were always books about the Adirondacks strewn about the place. For some reason, they always drew me like a magnet. At some point, the thought came to me that I should write about my own Adirondack adventures. These tales are as true as my memory and the memory of my sources (relatives) will allow. They are not in any particular order, just random stories to pass the time on a rainy day in the Adirondacks.

The author and his wife, Terri

Kayak Adventures

Before modern whitewater rafting outfitters came along, there were old-fashioned die-hard whitewater enthusiasts that would tie down their canoes and kayaks on the top of their car and hit the back woods roads seeking river access. There were no formal guides to cover the basic paddle strokes, or give their safety-first pitch, or line the group up for a bucket list photo. There were no flatbed trucks to pick you and your boat up at the end of the run and there certainly wasn't a professional briefing of the course, complete with a teamwork pep talk. Often there would be someone in the group who had paddled the river before, but sometimes it was just an old-fashioned adventure. If there was an experienced paddler, their pre-trip pep talk consisted of "paddle like hell and avoid the rocks." Packing a lifejacket, Converse sneakers, a bag lunch and a change of clothes, I was one of those old-school enthusiasts.

Living in the Adirondacks in the 1970s, I would often venture to North Hudson in the spring to observe the Whitewater Derby. Climbing over rocks and sliding down the sides of boulders along the shoreline of the Hudson River added to the total experience of watching the race. Canoes and kayaks, with their paddlers dressed in a wide array of colorful hats, helmets and lifejackets, were maneuvered through the icy water around rocks and over waterfalls. Some folks were frantically using an empty bleach jug to bail out their boat, some just gave up and carelessly floated by, while a few were counting their paddle strokes in unison on a mission to win the race. Occasionally, by the days end, an empty, half-sunken, banged-up aluminum canoe would float by, bobbing its way down the river towards Warrensburg. The fiberglass models didn't "bob" so much, so their shattered remnants just drifted by. It left me wondering what type of adventure took place to leave a boat in such destruction that someone would just let their prized possession float away. Maybe in some cases they didn't have a choice, with the current quickly pulling the craft from their cold, wet hands and others, like flinging one's golf clubs into the pond out of frustration, had just had enough of the sport and let the thing go. Either way, it seemed very stoic to watch the boats float by as the daylight turned to dusk—a bagpipe serenade would have been fitting to pay tribute to the passing debris.

Leaving the finish line was a mishmash of soaked paddlers with sweaty hair still in the form of a helmet, wet soggy pants and their sneakers going squish-squish as they walked across the dusty parking lot. Each beaten-down racer, carrying their war club disguised as a paddle, sought out their finishing time from some sort of official. I never knew anyone who knew exactly how the scoring system worked, or what it meant as everyone just looked at the faded and chipped plywood board for their name and their time. It looked like the organizers had dragged the board out of a pole barn from previous year's races and set it there, not bothering to change the names of the winners and certainly not bothering to change the finish times. Occasionally, there would be some fresh black marker on the board that gave cause for a comment, but what about all those other times? Could it be they had the same time every year? Most folks thought of it as a moral victory to even cross the finish line while still in their boat. Yet deep down, everyone wanted to brag, to get a trophy, a certificate, something to signify they had won. I can't recall ever sticking around to see who won a race. I'm not sure *anyone* ever stuck around to see who won. Strangely, everyone wanted to win but no one cared who did win.

Having only paddled my homemade kayak in the calm flat water of local ponds and lakes, I was yearning to crossover to the whitewater and get into the same action I had observed a few years prior on the Hudson. What I lacked in self-confidence I made up for in the trust I had in my kayak. I knew three layers of fiberglass and resin with a reinforced seat would hold up to any boulder encounter. Today's Kevlar and polymer kayaks and canoes are sleek and stylish. In the Seventies, they were in their early design stages and most kayaks were fiberglass and canoes were either fiberglass or aluminum. Nimble and light, fiberglass proved to be a worthy material for racing vessels as well as reliable for general recreation. I can attest to the reliability as I still use the fiberglass canoe my Uncle Allan and I constructed in 1975. Being a member of the Schenectady Winter Sports Club, Uncle Allan had many friends in the business of boatbuilding. One of his friends, Paul, had a heated garage filled with boatmaking materials.

Not only were there assorted boat molds, fiberglass cloth and a tank of resin, but there were serious kayaking enthusiasts hanging around who offered their expertise and opinions. Also essential was the little black and white television in the corner of the shop by the woodstove. Even seasoned boat-builders were never too busy to watch the Giants on Sunday afternoons. Henceforth came my first kayak as well as my Jenson racing canoe, which at 17' long and 48 pounds, would still match up with any modern day, commercially made racing canoe. The nice thing about the fiberglass boats was that they were easy to repair—simply throw a patch of fiberglass on the crack or hole or, in some instances, tack on a piece of duct tape! In whitewater circles, these are signs of battle or a novice paddler, but to the casual observer at a family campground in the Adirondacks it just looked like I lived frugally, not wanting to upgrade to a new boat.

The maiden voyage was an overnight paddle on Long Lake with Uncle Allan and his girls. As the hot mid-summer sun twinkled on the water, we unloaded our boats and gear onto the beach. Starting at the head of the lake, we paddled several miles north to a camping spot on its eastern shore. I misjudged how hot I would get paddling and began sweating early into the trip. As my arms started tiring, we finally spotted a rough clearing that was barely visible from the lake. Officially considered a 'primitive' campsite, it had a fire pit and a brown and yellow official state sign designating it a camping area. It was a nice break-in paddle of about six miles on flat water as opposed to the whitewater of a fast-flowing river. The only thrill to ease the pain of my tired arms was to dodge the wakes of the passing speed boats. Since I had to stuff my overnight camping gear into the kayak, I packed very sparsely, only bringing a sleeping bag and some snacks for the summer overnight trip. Of course, being in the Adirondacks, it rained that night and I was ill-prepared. My uncle and cousins slept soundly in their tents. I do believe I was instructed to bring a tent as well. As I laid in my wet sleeping bag on the patch of damp moss that I used as a mattress, I began doubting if I was cut out for these types of adventures. It was a learning experience to say the least, but don't try and pass that off to a 14-year-old.

Soon after the break-in voyage, we began to paddle on Kayaderosseras Creek in Rock City Falls for fun day trips. There were two sections of the creek and we stuck to the upper section, which was basically fast-moving water without the rocks and waterfalls. Uncle Allan thought I was ready to enter the Kayaderosseras Derby and I was led to believe that, as a novice, I only needed to complete the upper portion of the race, the part of which I was familiar.

I was dropped off at the starting point by my dad and he drove off to meet me at the finish line. As I was steadying my kayak in the creek, a race official shouted out my name. He waved me out of my boat and motioned for me to meet with some official-looking folks with pins and patches on their hats, kind of like being called to the vice-principal's office. I was thinking that my equipment didn't meet the race criteria, or my hockey helmet didn't meet the race specifications. I quickly found out that, being only 14, I needed a parent's signature on the race waiver. Apparently, we had overlooked that part of the paperwork. My dad had already driven off to the finish line, 12 miles down the road, and this was decades before cell phones were even a thought. I must have drawn the compassion of the race official (unlike the vice-principal) because he conveniently asserted his official authority on another pressing matter and quickly looked away as I forged my dad's signature on the waiver.

It was the first time I ever forged my dad's name—it wasn't the last. I learned that forgery worked on progress reports from the junior high as well. Heck, if it passed on something as significant as a whitewater race waiver, what would be the harm to do it on a measly report card? I guess if I worked my way into a life of crime by forging checks, I could blame it all on a volunteer kayak race official. I quickly climbed back into my kayak and began paddling, confident I would finish somewhere in the top ten—after all, it was my first race. When I got to the halfway point, I realized there was no one there to meet me and the race was for the entire length of the creek, into the unventured waters where I had never been. In the few times I had paddled that creek, we always got out at the halfway point and looked at what we called the 'dangerous waters of the abyss' lurking ahead. As I looked down stream, all I could see was fast-moving water and rock formations. I wondered what the sense was in signing up as a novice when this race was obviously for experts. I had no choice but to continue with the race. For the first time in my life I pushed myself out of my comfort zone. I was scared, but I finished the race, not in the top ten as I had confidently predicted, but, humbly, in the top 100. I felt a new level of self-confidence that I had never had before and when I showed up back home with wet clothes and a scratched boat, the neighbors thought I was an expert kayaker.

Now that I had mastered the Kayaderosseras Creek, it was time to take on the Hudson River as a participant instead of as a spectator.

As I sat in my kayak, grasping onto the rocky shoreline of the Hudson river and listening to the roar of the charging water, I thought, *this current is a lot stronger than it looked from the road.* I waited in numerical order behind a row of sleek, commercially made boats waiting for the number on my bib to be called. Wearing my life jacket and my hockey helmet, I felt slightly (if not majorly) intimidated, by the older, better-outfitted kayakers buoying in front of me with their superior kayaks, fancy helmets, and curved paddles. The racer's number in front of me was called and he was off and through the first gate, looking like he was prepping for an Olympic tryout. His equipment matched his skills, smooth and sleek. I re-evaluated my set up and began wondering if I wasn't in a little over my head. With paddle in hand, I waited for my number to be called over the public-address system. To my surprise and embarrassment, the announcer blurted out, "Good luck, John!" Apparently, unbeknownst to me, my friend's dad was the official race starter and, recognizing my outfit and the force of the current, thought it might be the last words I'd ever hear. He most likely wanted to say, "Get the heck out of there!" but off I went.

The object was to navigate through 'gates' that were metal poles dangling over the river and planted into the shoreline with cables. These gates were strategically hung near tricky drop-offs and swirling eddies to make it more difficult to pass through without touching the gate. To touch a gate, even with the slightest ding, meant you lost points. After slapping the first three gates hard with my kayak, discouragement immediately set in. I could see the stern-looking judges sitting on the rocks quickly marking off my deficiencies on their clipboards. I then had to cross the river to get to the next gate. Using every bit of arm strength I could muster, I crossed the river and promptly banged into that gate as well. At this point, my focus was not to navigate the stupid gates but to just get down the river. I promptly cruised past the next gate and all the remaining gates. I passed by the other kayakers, whom I could see out of the corner of my eye, and took the easiest course through the rocks. I'm sure the other racers and judges were thinking, *What is that kid doing?* I felt relieved to reach the finish line and get out of my boat. The relief was only temporary, however, because when the other kayakers started coming to shore I could feel their glares at the kid with a hockey helmet and homemade boat who had just paddled past them skipping all the gates. I was sure they were thinking, *Doesn't that punk know the rules?* Or, they could have been thinking worse things like, *What a loser!* I received 28 penalty points for the race, which, in my book, gave me a passing grade.

My ordeal on the Hudson didn't deter me from my quest to move up from being a novice kayaker to a top finisher. By the next spring, my Uncle Allen had persuaded me to enter the Sacandaga River race in Lake Luzerne. After all, the other guys back at the boatbuilding garage did this gig all the time. Over the winter, I took a class on how to do an Eskimo roll in a kayak. I was prepared to show my stuff but secretly hoped I wouldn't run into any of the fellas from the Hudson Whitewater derby or from the Schenectady Winter sports club.

As I paddled through the speedy rapids, I was greatly encouraged when I made it through the first two gates without touching them. I nodded to the judges on the shoreline in a show of pride. I thought maybe a year of gaining some weight and building up arm strength was starting to matter. I was sure I weighed at least 140 pounds. With my adrenaline pumping and confidence flowing, I had my sight set on the next gate off in the distance. Cradled along the shoreline I could see a crowd of spectators staring at the gate. I thought, *Why all the attention to that gate?* From up river it looked like a simple pass through, so I thought, *I'll show off my new-found skills. They'll think twice about mocking the kid in the homemade boat with the hockey helmet.* In a matter of seconds, I was flipped under my boat, totally submerged in the raging river. I believe any kayaker will tell you that the instinct to breathe takes over and you will quickly figure out how to get air. Which is what I did, grabbing the pull string on the skirt of the boat, and quickly pulling myself to the surface of the river. I couldn't understand why the Eskimo roll class I took at the YMCA, in the heated pool with two instructors holding the boat, didn't work for me in the ice-cold raging river. Holding tightly to my flipped-over kayak and paddle I floated down river to the finish line feeling fortunate that I was wearing my homemade wet suit. As I floated past the other racers who were navigating their way through the gates, I was sure they were thinking, *There goes that kid again!*

The Upper Hudson is a fierce, fast-moving, generally clean, picturesque river whose origins are from melting snow and rain-filled streams. As you get further downstream, the river changes color and velocity, eventually ending in New York City and the Atlantic Ocean. Once the Hudson departs the Adirondack Park, it quickly takes on a different persona. So much so, in fact, that there used to be a kayak race in Fort Edward, New York called the Sludge Water Derby, named for the color and texture the water took on after it passed through the paper mills in Glens Falls. The race was kind of like a church picnic softball game, but for kayakers, especially those who wanted to compete but were not at the level they used to be, or ever were. Entering the Sludge Water Derby was my only hope in my quest to prove my kayaking ability. After all, I was a seasoned teenage kayaker with three races under his belt and no trophies to show for it. Surely, I would have an advantage in a race that involved sludge. As I dragged my kayak off the car top and across the muddy parking lot to the edge of the shoreline, I noticed a stale, almost musty smell in the air. After getting situated in my boat and seeing the brown murky water, I realized the musty smell was coming from the river itself. This wasn't the Adirondacks! Instead of a rocky shoreline with tall pine trees, fresh air and chirping birds, it was a muddy shoreline with rusty pipes, an obnoxious smell and a few creepy-looking crows lurking from dead branches. I had heard that the papermill and pigment factories had polluted the river with toxic PCBs, but I had never gotten close enough to notice or care about it. Now I was sitting in it.

A revelation came to me when I realized there were only four kayakers entered in the race. *Oh man,* I thought, *I only need to beat one of these guys to finish third and get a trophy.* I was psyched! Obviously, I had lowered my expectations based upon the results of my previous races. Being that there were only four of us, we all started the race at once and it was a simple 'first one to the finish line wins.' I could tell that the other three guys were there together as some sort of Sunday afternoon bonding event. I was sure they were thinking, *Maybe the kid with the homemade kayak and hockey helmet belongs here but we don't.* I'm sure they pegged me as a local kid. There was definitely no 'brotherhood of kayakers' present at this race. Even in a redneck kayak race I was an outcast. At least one of the guys was decent enough to grunt out, "Good luck kid."

It was a very hot summer day which made the stench of the water and the muddy shoreline even more pronounced. The informal official starter sounded the blowhorn and we were off. Halfway into the race the three dudes, with their sleek slalom racing boats and extravagant lifejackets, had a sizeable lead as their rhythmical paddle strokes made it look effortless. There was no doubt that this race was 'chump change' for them, probably just an outing to try out their new paddles or just to add some hardware to their trophy case.

Then suddenly, and without logic, fate took over—the kayaker in front of me flipped over. There was no whitewater. There were no eddies. No sudden drop-off. The only logic I could think of was that he got dizzy from the combination of the hot sun and the toxic fumes evaporating from the river.

The shock of having his body submerged in the polluted water drove him to quickly drag his kayak to the shore. As I paddled past him, I could see his obvious disgust as he ripped off his helmet and what was once a colorful life jacket to clean himself up. My first thought was, *I wonder how many toxins that guy ingested?* My second thought was, *I'm breaking out for the finish line before he figures out that I passed him.* As he watched me paddle by, he quickly gathered up his gear, wiped the glaze of mercury toxins off his life vest and pushed his way out of the mud. By then I had a hundred-yard lead on him. One hundred yards quickly became fifty yards, then thirty yards, and each time I glanced back I could see the grit and determination on his face and in the force of his paddle strokes. I decided it was best to stop looking back. I could gauge the distance between us by watching his buddies' reactions at the finish line ahead. I paddled as hard as I could as sweat poured out under from my helmet, which with its padding for hockey, was obviously designed for cold weather usage. This was now a two-man race. One man wanting a trophy in the worst way and one man not wanting to be embarrassed by losing a race to a scrawny local kid in a homemade boat.

As I crossed the finish line a few boat lengths ahead of my competitor, I dared not look back. I did not want to encourage any after-race altercation. I heard him mumble something as his friends asked him why his boat flipped. I humbly paddled to shore and unassumingly pulled my boat out of the water, tied it to the top of my car and gathered up my belongings. There were no spectators or family members there to celebrate, just me, knowing I had finished third. I was excited as I made my way over to the scorer's table with great anticipation of humbly accepting my hard-earned third place trophy. Apparently, due to the low budget of the event, they didn't issue trophies. No plaque, no certificate, not a note in the local newspaper, nothing! The only evidence I had that I had even entered the race was my cloth racing bib, which I was supposed to turn over to the race sponsor. Pent-up frustration can cause a man to take risks and make irrational decisions. I was at my breaking point. I stuffed the bib, with the #6 imprinted on it, into my kayak and out of sight from the race official. There was no way I was leaving Fort Edward without some sort of evidence I finished third. The bib hung in my bedroom at home for the next year. Then it hung in my first apartment. Then it hung in the basement of my first house. Any time anyone made note of it, I proudly proclaimed my third-place finish in a whitewater kayak race in the mighty Hudson River.

The bib and the hockey helmet eventually got packed up in a box and went the way of my Nolan Ryan baseball card and G.I. Joe action figures as lost treasures. My homemade fiberglass kayak was eventually sold, and my whitewater racing days went the way of the sunken boats on the Upper Hudson.

I think I heard bagpipes playing as the guy drove off with my kayak on his car.

Black Bears

Lake Eaton is one of the Adirondack Park's most popular family campgrounds. Located just outside the village of Long Lake, it has a long and storied past, not only with my family but with countless others seeking the Adirondack family camping experience. Over the years, Lake Eaton has evolved to meet the needs of the modern family, including updated toilet facilities and a shower building. To the casual 'car camping' family, Lake Eaton represents the picturesque campground of postcard lore, with spacious tent sites, a playground and a sprawling sandy beach, all overlooking Owl's Head Mountain on the opposite side of the lake. However, as anyone who has camped in the Adirondacks can testify, there is a price to pay for the serenity and relaxation. Whether it be thunder and lightning storms, mosquitoes, black flies and deer flies biting at your ankles, or a neighbor's barking dog, annoyance does cut its way into the postcard. After all, that's part of the total Adirondack experience.

From the early 1960s until the early 1980s, Adirondack campgrounds had one major flaw, the infamous, green-metal trash can, which was eventually eradicated due to modern recycling methods—the current regulations were to encourage people to take their trash home with them. No more trips to the dump and no more garbage trucks making their daily rounds. The dented green metal trash cans seemed to fit into the whole thematic experience: the trash collectors in stained t-shirts with sweaty bandannas on their heads and a cigarette hanging from their lip, jogging after the beat-up trash truck sporting the town emblem on the door and all of it supplying the daily morning entertainment in the campground.

Those simple rustic metal cans had one major drawback—they attracted black bears. It wasn't so much the color of the cans, since most of the green paint had worn off to expose the rust, but what was inside the cans that was so attractive to the bears.

In Long Lake there is a town dump that in the 1970s was basically a large open trash pit—a pit that got "stirred" by tractors and bulldozers after periodic dumping. During the warm summer evenings, as dusk was settling on the Adirondacks, black bears would make their way to the dump to feast on remnants from the campgrounds and from the village residents. On any given evening, there would be 12 to 20 black bears pawing around the dump.

In the 1970s there was less regulation regarding dump sites, and anyone could freely "walk among the bears" if one so desired. Although I did observe a guy tossing some marshmallows at one of the smaller bears, most folks kept their distance, though not necessarily a safe one. I figured we just had to be faster than the kid standing next to us. You would listen for a twig to snap or the rustle of some underbrush and soon another bear would emerge from the surrounding woods to paw through the trash. Even though 20 to 30 people would be observing the bears, there was always an eerie silence as if not to disturb the bears while they were dining. An occasional "ooh" or "ahh" would break the silence if a larger bear were to make its way out of the woods like a famous wrestler making his way down the aisle to the center ring. The observance ritual would end when it started to get dark or if it started to rain. No one wanted to be on the wrong path back to their car in the dark while hungry bears lurked nearby.

Back at Lake Eaton, campfires dotted the shoreline around the lake as the cool Adirondack night set in. Family campfires have always been the focal point of any camping trip. After an evening of toasting marshmallows and sharing ghost stories, my family settled into our tents for the night. It was not long after settling down that we heard two guys yelling at the campsite across from us. The campsites were anywhere from 10 yards to 20 yards from each other so there wasn't much to decipher—they were yelling at a black bear. Apparently, these inexperienced campers had left their food sitting in the back of their pickup truck and the bear had climbed into the bed of the truck. What happened next could only have happened in the 1970s. One of the guys took out his gun and shot the bear dead in his tracks on the road between campsites. If someone were to shoot a gun in a campground today, I'm confident there would be State Police helicopters and local law enforcement on site within minutes, and maybe a few animal rights activists, but on that night, no one noticed except our family, lying in our nearby tents. The next morning the Conservation Department workers came and loaded the bear into the back of a truck, carted it off to a remote field and buried it, assuming that it had died of natural causes. One of the crew who was loading the bear onto the truck made a comment about the bear "getting into something."

My Uncle Bruce, who happened to be the forest ranger at Long Lake at the time, stopped by for the family campfire the next night. When we started telling him the story of the "shots being fired" at the bear, he looked astonished. He was told by his conservation crew that the bear had died of natural causes, most likely from eating out of trash cans. The next morning, he took that same crew out to the remote field and dug up the bear. Upon examining the bear, he found the bullet slug and the investigation began to track down the "armed camper."

The gunslinging camper, realizing his stupidity, checked out of the campground and headed home to wait for the sheriff to knock on his door.

The following summer, after attending a Boy Scout jamboree in Saratoga County, my Uncle Mack and I headed up to Lake Eaton to meet up with other family members who had secured several campsites at the campground. Accompanying us was 20 pounds of macaroni salad in a jumbo-size foil tray, a leftover from the jamboree. Of course, after sitting out in the hot sun of the jamboree and enduring a two-hour ride in the trunk of Mack's car from Glens Falls to Lake Eaton, the macaroni salad was not safe for human consumption. Uncle Mack thought it was "perfectly fine" but other family members, after careful examination, deemed it "too risky" to eat. The spoiled salad, tray and all, ended up in the green metal trash can on the road edge of the campsite. Why no one gave any thought to it attracting bears goes beyond reason, for later that night a very large 500-pound black bear sat at the edge of the campsite, gorging on the macaroni salad but leaving behind the crumpled aluminum pan. The Boy Scouts wouldn't eat it, my family wouldn't touch it, but it was a delicacy to that bear who could now cancel a trip to the dump.

Most summers, we would camp with relatives or family friends. It became a family tradition to camp at Lake Eaton. Among those relatives were my Aunt Glenda, Uncle Dave and Cousin Glen, who had recently moved back to the area after living in England for several years. Uncle Dave had an English-built car with leather seats and a sleek body; he loved the car so much that he had it transported with him when they moved back to the U.S. He called it his "English Rover." It was in this car that they arrived to camp with us at Lake Eaton that summer.

* * * * *

My Uncle Dave was well known within our family for his famous teriyaki sauce. He didn't let us down, cooking up a delicious meal that night that drew glimpses from neighboring campers wondering what the sweet-smelling smoke was coming from. Not wanting to waste the leftover sauce, he placed it securely in a plastic container and put it into the trunk of his Rover for the night.

Early the next morning, just as the sky started getting light, my cousin and I were woken up by three growling bears several yards from our little two-person tent. As we gently unzipped the nylon tent door flap, we observed the largest of the three bears circling my uncle's car. The bear was sniffing all around the car.

We lay perfectly still not wanting to draw attention to our defenseless state. I wondered about the cheese and crackers I had brought into the tent when we went to bed. Pondering how a cotton sleeping bag would hold up to a bear's claws I decided to slip on my sneakers in case I needed to run. I then heard my uncle from his nearby tent whisper, "don't move boys." For once, two teenage boys were in full agreement with a parent. The large black bear then climbed up on the trunk of the English car and started clawing at the trunk, trying desperately to get to the teriyaki sauce. The bear began rocking the car back and forth in an effort to pry off the trunk.

After 20 minutes the large bear gave up his efforts and the other two bears lost interest as well. They slowly moved on, leaving large gashes on the truck of my uncle's car. Uncle Dave's insurance agent didn't believe the story and tried to deny his insurance claim, noting the expense at getting a new trunk shipped from England.

Lake Eaton is still a great family campground, but the black bear adventures are nowhere near what they used to be. Bears are now discouraged from meandering around state camp-grounds. There is no more leftover macaroni salad from the Boy Scout jamboree; there is no more teriyaki sauce in the trunk of the English car; and the dented green metal trash cans are long gone. The Long Lake town dump is no longer a des-tination for bears or people. Certainly, black bears remain a part of the Adirondack experience as they still seek out dump-sters and picnic baskets, but the lure of those dented, rusty, green trash cans is now just a part of the park's history.

Winter Camping

Sam was snoring so loud he could have stirred the local black bears out of their winter hibernation. It wasn't the loudness of his snoring that aggravated me, it was the fact that he was able to sleep at all in the bitter cold winter night. I sat shivering and shaking fiercely with my sleeping bag, which seemed useless in providing any warmth whatsoever, wrapped around me. As I prayed that I would not freeze to death, I envisioned Sam waking up in the morning, finding my frozen body in a prone position on the floor of the lean-to, shrugging his shoulders and continuing with the hike. As I pondered Sam's lack of compassion for his frozen friend, I fought to stay awake. I thought of all the other successful winter camping trips I had experienced. How did it all come to this?

My earliest adventure in winter camping started when I was 12 years old. I had joined my dad and his buddies on their annual winter camping trip to Stephen's Pond. They had done this trip for several years and my dad thought I was now ready for the trek. Being the youngster among the "old-timers," I was granted a fair amount of grace on the hike and, at times, was used as an excuse for these gents to take extra breaks themselves, not wanting to admit to their peers that they were tired or hungry. As we crossed Lake Durant on our snowshoes, the icy wind swept across the lake cutting into my face and neck. As I wrapped my scarf over my face, I began to wonder why I was doing this. At least when I went sledding, I had the option of sitting in the car to warm up. On this hike, we had three more miles to go to an open-air lean-to. I thought back to the last few weeks and the anticipation I had built up for the hike. The planning phase of the trip made it all sound fun and exciting. The older guys would corner my dad after church and come up with a new idea for the hike, such as leaving earlier in the morning, staying an extra night or discussing the style of snowshoe that would work best. Would it be the Bear Paws this year or the Michigans?

The enthusiasm of the older guys drew me in and they found snowshoes perfect for a rookie winter camper like me. Even the car ride to Lake Durant stirred my excitement as we stopped at a shop in Indian Lake to pick up some "extras" for the hike, like candy bars and film.

Once we got off the frozen lake and into the cover of the trees, the wind died down and the hike became more bearable. The old-timers noted the beauty of the fresh fallen snow on the tree branches and the crispness of the air. All I noticed was that my legs were getting heavy and I was hungry. I wasn't used to hiking in snowshoes while also being weighed down with snow pants, a heavy winter jacket and a backpack with my sleeping bag and extra clothes. I kept my metal Boy Scout issue canteen strapped to my belt hoping the "herky-jerky" motion of walking on snowshoes would prevent my drinking water from freezing solid. The three-mile hike seemed more like ten miles and, since this was all new to me, I had no way of knowing how far we had progressed except to continually ask the others. "'Bout halfway" was the standard reply.

Once we arrived at the lean-to, we mapped out our sleeping arrangements by unrolling our bags and staging our back packs. It seemed to me that the old-timers were particular about where they set up, so I waited to claim my space and wondered what it was going to be like sleeping amongst a group of old men. We scavenged around the woods for any low-hanging branches or barren logs to start a fire and Myron and Paul debated the best method of building the fire. Myron, an avid hiker who hiked well into his eighties, thought using some lint and bits of birch bark would be proper. "Best to keep with tradition" was Myron's plea as he pulled out some lint wadded up in a flannel cloth. Paul, looking like an Adirondack guide with his suspenders, felt hat, gray beard and wool pants, simply said, "I'll use some lighter fluid and a match," which he conveniently pulled out of his pack. Being the middle of February and in the woods near a frozen pond, there was not much to keep a 12-year-old entertained. After venturing as far as I dared from the lean-to on my own, I soon realized my only source of entertainment was listening to the old-timers comparing hiking stories. You would have thought they were the founding fathers of the Adirondack Park negotiating with Indian Chiefs and British Officials for land rights.

Preparing meals in a snow-covered camp site in the freezing cold took a lot of patience. To prepare a meal, there first had to be a fire—not just any fire, but one with the right balance of coals and flame. The meals were simple enough: They consisted mostly of hot dogs, can soup, oatmeal and spam. To be a part of the team, I took on the duty of continually melting snow into water to be heated for instant coffee, hot chocolate and cleaning up. Melting snow kept me occupied and out of the way of the "seniors." Myron had brought a pistol with him, which provided entertainment as each old-timer took a turn shooting at a pea soup can mounted on a log at the edge of the frozen pond.

When it got dark, we congregated in the lean-to. My dad looked at his Timex watch and mentioned, surprisingly, that it was only 8:00. Paul and Cuthbart, a tall stoic man with suspenders and protruding eyebrows, pulled out their pipes and tobacco and sat on the edge of the lean-to smoking. Cuthbart, or "Cut" as they called him, began telling stories of lost hikers and mysterious occurrences in the area, I'm sure for my benefit. I began to get the impression he didn't want me on the hike and that I was intruding on the old-timer's weekend away.

Just as we were settled in, a group of snowmobiles drove past the lean-to with their engines roaring and headlights casting huge shadows through the trees. The old-timers were annoyed that the serene silence of the night was so rudely interrupted by the inconsiderate "snowmobilers." They all mumbled and grunted with a few colorful terms mixed in. My first thought was, *Why couldn't we have used snowmobiles on this trip?* I thought of asking my dad if one of the snowmobilers could give me a lift to the car the next day, but I didn't think that would go over too well with this group so I just kept that thought to myself, although I was secretly tempted to say it anyway just to annoy Cuthbart.

Going to the bathroom in the outdoors in the winter proved to be no easy task and one that didn't come to mind until we set up camp and I noticed there was no outhouse at Stephen's Pond. This became especially tricky while wearing snowshoes. I tried to hike to a private spot far enough away from the lean-to to "do my duty" only to realize without the snowshoes I sank up to my thighs in snow. I didn't know how the others did it and I wasn't about to ask. That surely would have brought a grin to Cuthbart.

Once we got back to the parking lot at Lake Durant, I reluctantly asked the Ranger's wife if I could use the bathroom in their house. "It's kind of an emergency," I mumbled. I needed a real bathroom. Of course, it became a big production as everyone wondered what the "emergency" was. The nice lady chided the old-timers saying, "That young kid hiked all the way in with you?" She seemed impressed with my accomplishment, which encouraged me. The old-timers thought it best not to challenge the Ranger's wife about her inquiry.

* * * * *

After a couple of "break in" winter camping trips to Stephen's Pond, my dad thought we were ready to tackle a "serious" winter camping trip to the high peaks. Dad always carefully studied the trail maps and route details when planning our trips. He would lay out topographic maps side by side on our dining room table and review the best routes to take. On paper, they looked exciting and achievable. Of course, that was sitting in our warm and cozy dining room eating ice cream, far, far away from being wet, cold and exhausted.

We both agreed to join the Adirondack Mountain Club on a hike up Haystack Mountain and stay at a lean-to at Bushnell Falls, somewhere past John's Brook Lodge. It was foreign territory to my dad and I, but it sure looked good on the trail maps. This was the first (and last) time that we hiked with a group of strangers. They weren't relatives or people from the church. *What if they were really fit and blazed on ahead to leave us straggling or worse yet, what if we were the cause of slowing down the pace of the hike? Would we be rejected by the club?* The thought hung with us during the weeks leading up to the trip.

We prepared as best as we could, lightening our metal-frame hiking packs by only packing dry food such as oatmeal, hot cocoa mix, instant potatoes and trail mix. My pack still felt heavy, especially to take on a hike up a high peak on snowshoes. I repacked several times and removed as much as I could from the pack based upon my own reasoning.

We car-pooled from Glens Falls, with the guys in the one car and the ladies in a van, to the Garden parking lot in Keene where we started hiking. The Adirondack Mountain Club group ended up being a very diverse group of hikers of varied ability and personalities. The leader, Ron, happened to be someone my dad knew and was obviously a high-level, experienced hiker. His son, who was in his early 20s, and his son's friend, were evidently there on a mission because as soon as they climbed out of the back of the car they proclaimed, "Let's conquer this thing."

The remainder of the group were women. Ron's wife, Ron's wife's friend, Ron's wife's friend's friend, etc. . . . My dad and I were the ones that "didn't quite fit in." When we arrived at the Garden parking lot in Keene, it was briskly cold but picturesque, with the sun twinkling through the trees. Each hiker carefully prepared their scarfs and hats, shifted their snow pants and tightened their boot straps before attaching their snow shoes. It was a colorful collage of nylon coats, wool hats and assorted hiking gear.

The hike to the lean-to went as planned, and as the group began to chat along the trail, some comradery took place. Taking breaks in the hiking seemed to flow naturally among the varied levels of hikers. My dad and I breathed a sigh of relief that we were of equal ability with most of the group.

Once we arrived at the lean-to at Bushnell Falls, the customary "claiming of the sleeping spot" took place. Since I now understood the process, I just waited it all out and laid my sleeping bag down in the empty spot that remained. One of the go-getters got a fire started, and I started scouting out the area. The snow was very deep, so I wasn't going far off the beaten path. I was encouraged to find an outhouse at this camp, especially since we were in mixed company. Apparently, the Adirondack Mountain Club took hygiene into consideration, unlike the Stephen's Pond gang.

I wandered over to the nearby creek that roared as it flowed briskly down the side of the mountain. Along the shores of the creek were little patches of ice where the water had pooled and allowed a thin layer of ice to form. The ice patches intrigued me. I wanted to know just how thin this layer of ice was, so I began to push against the ice with my right hand. With a "crack" my hand broke through the ice and my leather glove quickly filled with icy water. I knew in an instant that I was in trouble, as I recalled leaving my extra mittens at home to lighten my pack.

As I made my way back to the camp, I thought of different stories I could tell my dad about what happened. Once I spied the campfire in front of the lean-to, I figured I would just dry my glove by the fire and hope no one would notice. I put my soaking wet leather glove on a stick and wedged it between some rocks on the back edge of the firepit. Then, casually, I just kept my right hand in my pocket and hoped my dad wouldn't notice my missing glove. We were eating dinner and everything was going according to plan when one of the women in the group proclaimed, "someone's glove is burning!"

It then became the focal point of the entire camp. Sheepishly claiming my glove, I held the charred, partially wet glove in my hand, telling my dad exactly what had happened. I think the guilt of not bringing any spare gloves himself made him feel sorry for me. Having just provided the dinner entertainment for the camp, I was hoping I would never see any of these folks again after the hike was over. Then Ron stepped up and proudly proclaimed, "I have extra gloves." as he handed me the warmest, most expensive pair of gloves I'd ever worn. Ron's "heroic" actions only brought confirmation to the group that he had his act together and I didn't.

The next morning it became obvious that there was a great divide in the group. There were those who wanted to scale Haystack Mountain on their snowshoes and there were those who wouldn't even considering doing it. It was a brief discussion. The leader, Ron, politely gave my dad and I the option of joining him and the guys to climb Haystack or to join the ladies hiking back to the car and going home. Everyone in the group already knew the answer and rudely gawked at us as we discussed our options. I'm sure that was one time where my dad used my youth as an excuse for not doing something he really didn't want to do. In his mind, my dad would have loved to do it so he could tell folks back home he climbed Haystack Mountain on snowshoes, but he knew, and I knew, we were both out of our league. We packed up and sheepishly hiked back to the van with the ladies. My dad and I sat in the third seat of the van as the women applied their Chap Stick and mussed with their hair and chatted all the way home. My long underwear was damp and my clothes smelled like smoke. I was very hungry, very tired and could not think of one thing that was fun about the hike. It was getting more 'unfun' every minute as we sat in the back of that van. I could not get home soon enough! At least with the Stephen's Pond hike, it was just the old-timers and they usually smelled worse than me at the end of the camping trip.

I was well into my thirties when my hiking buddy, Sam, said, "We should do a winter camping trip to the high peaks."

"Of course we should," I confidently replied. After all, by then I was an 'old pro' when it came to winter camping. I quickly referenced my campouts with the Boy Scouts and the Adirondack Mountain club, conveniently leaving out my misfortunes. I acted as if the Conservation Department itself was begging me to go on staff as their official "Winter Camping Director."

Sam for some reason was infatuated with Marcy Dam. We had hiked there in the summer and climbed Mount Marcy with some success, so I guess Sam wanted to see the Dam in the winter season. Our plan was to backpack into Marcy Dam, set up camp in a lean-to and then hike up Phelps Mountain. I had climbed Phelps on snowshoes with my dad and his friend, Gary, when I was in my teens. I assured Sam that Phelps Mountain, although a high peak, was climbable in the winter. Sam's 13-year-old son, Geoffrey, joined us on our hike, which prompted us to go while he was on winter break from school.

Sam insisted that we go prepared for the worst, so we packed so many "extras" that we had to pull a toboggan loaded with camping gear. Pulling a toboggan while wearing snow shoes and carrying a back pack proved no easy task, which is probably why we had never seen anyone else do it. We extended a rope in the front of the toboggan so it wouldn't roll over our snow shoes and attached another rope to the back of the toboggan so it wouldn't roll downhill away from us. By our estimate the sled weighed over 60 pounds. There was a cooler with a jug of water for coffee, eggs and bacon for breakfast, a lantern, Coleman fuel for the lantern, a box of dry food, a spare tent (in case the lean-to was full), a frying pan, a coffee pot and whatever else Sam thought we needed. Everything was tied down with rope. It looked heavy and it was heavy. It would have made any hillbilly family proud. The sky was clear, and with a slight breeze blowing through the trees, we assumed the 30-degree temperature would drop as we started hiking. By the time we reached Marcy Dam with the toboggan, we were sweaty and exhausted. We had miscalculated the effort that it would take to pull the sled the three miles from the parking lot to the dam.

Fortunately, there were two empty lean-tos at the campsite, and we didn't have to try putting up a tent in several feet of snow. Being that there were only three of us, we skipped the pecking order ritual of "picking your lean-to spot" and just threw our packs and bags on the floor. Sam, cognizant of his loud snoring, said that he would sleep in the corner, as if it were a separate soundproof room.

Wood was tough to come by, so we scoured the area around the dam looking for broken twigs to burn. The water that once flowed steadily over the dam was frozen solid in hues of grey and milky white, like an oversized comforter laying over the side of a bed. As the bright clear sky started fading to grey, the long haunting shadows from the desolate trees disappeared into the night and the temperature started dropping. In unison we spoke forth our thoughts, "How cold does it have to get for a waterfall to freeze?"

We stomped the snow down in the fire pit and carefully laid the few twigs we found over some paper plates and then coated it all with Coleman fuel. The instant flame quickly burnt away the paper plates, while leaving the frozen branches intact. The flame didn't last long enough to even warm our hands. We tried this routine a few more times before giving up, finally coming to the realization that frozen tree branches just won't burn.

After each of us took a turn visiting the outhouse, we took off our boots and wrapped ourselves into our sleeping bags, seeking warmth. I was sure that my red union suit and my goose down sleeping bag would keep me snug, thus ignoring Sam's idea of setting up the tent inside the lean-to. I left all my clothes on and curled up inside the bag hoping to warm it up. As the minutes turned to hours and without a fire to gaze at, I just lay there shivering while I thought of all the ways there were to die other than freezing to death. It was a long, long night. Sam, for some odd reason, thought to bring a "space blanket" with him. The paper-thin silver "blanket" looked more like a tablecloth than a blanket but when he stuffed it inside his sleeping bag it warmed him right up, enough to snore soundly. Geoffrey apparently had the same idea since he was sleeping as well.

As the frigid dark night turned to dawn, I attempted to put on my frozen boots that had been sitting next to me "chilling" for hours. Once I wedged them on, I made my way back to the frozen outhouse. Soon Sam and Geoffrey woke up to my rustling around the lean-to. After several attempts to start the Coleman stove, we came to the consensus that it was too cold for the stove to work, which meant no coffee and no breakfast. We checked the cooler only to find our eggs were frozen solid along with the water in the spare water jug. Just as we were discussing our "opportunities," a group of cross-country skiers from John's Brook Lodge skied up to the lean-to. After browsing over our campsite and seeing the toboggan and miscellaneous cooking supplies, along with the Coleman stove, one of them said with astonishment, "Did you sleep out here last night?" Before we could reply, he stated, "It was twenty-eight below zero!"

Without taking a vote, I said, "I've had enough. I'm going back to the car!" Sam and Geoffrey agreed even though they had gotten several more hours of sleep then me, but going without food and water was the deal breaker. We packed up our bedding and cooking supplies and loaded everything onto the toboggan and into our backpacks. Every activity was compounded by the frigid temperature and lack of sleep. Sucking down melted snow on our tongues, we wasted no time in hitting the trail back to the parking lot.

As we hiked the frozen trail back to the car, we quickly warmed up due to the heavy load we were carrying. Taking away sleep, food and water and compounding it with below zero temperatures left us all with "attitudes." After pulling the toboggan up a slight grade on the trail, we stopped to take a breath and to pull slightly off the trail to allow a group of cross-country skiers pass by. A lanky, arrogant-looking guy, nattily dressed in designer ski apparel, who was skiing along at a brisk pace, stopped abruptly and sarcastically stated, "Thanks, guys, for wearing snowshoes and ruining the ski trails!"

Being exhausted and dulled by the cold, his reproving words didn't really register with us at first. But as they sunk in, I'm certain that if there weren't witnesses on that trail, my short Italian friend would have left that guy buried headfirst in four feet of snow—and continued with the hike. Years later I am still reminded of the confrontation. "Can you believe that guy!" At least we didn't end the hike in the Lake Placid jail.

The author, at the right, on Stephen's Pond, 1972

Geoffrey, Sam and the author on the 28° below zero camping trip

Ice Hockey

Double runner skates, which have two steel blades instead of one, were standard issue in my family. The same pair of double runner hockey skates made their way through all four boys in our family. The skates were already well broken in when I, the oldest boy, inherited them, undoubtedly from an uncle or cousin. Not only did I have the very well-used double-bladed skates, but I was also required to wear ankle straps, which were simply pieces of leather with a buckle on the end, like miniature belts 18" to 24" long. The leather straps would be tightly wrapped around my ankles in order to give them more support and keep them from flopping sideways when I went on the ice. I was told by my dad that I needed the straps because I had "weak ankles," but there was never a thought given about the handed-down leather ice skates having no support structure whatsoever.

After donning my snow pants, winter jacket, scarf and New York Rangers knit cap, I was too bound up to put on my skates and the leather ankle straps so I simply left my legs laying across the vinyl kitchen floor waiting for my mom or my dad to attach everything to my feet. Since we only lived a short distance from the skating rink at Crandall Park, I would put on my skates at home, ride in the back seat of our station wagon, then trudge across the parking lot in all my apparel, climb over a snow bank and onto the ice joining a hundred other kids who undoubtedly had gone through a similar ritual.

It would be difficult to find anyone who grew up in the city of Glens Falls who couldn't tell you a story about Crandall Park. I personally spent many hours at Crandall Park engaging in a wide variety of outdoor activities, including: tennis, basketball, softball, sledding, rock concerts, fishing, Boy Scout meetings where we played capture the flag, work picnics and, most importantly, ice skating and hockey. Long before there were enclosed ice-skating rinks, Crandall Park was the place to go for ice skating. The city would plow the field, flood it using a fire hose and hang up flood lights around the park creating a very respectable, well-lit skating surface. They also erected a hockey box, flooding that in a similar manner.

Of course, the conditions of the ice and hockey rinks were dictated by the weather. A warm rainy day would make skating very difficult, yet it never seemed to hinder my determination to learn to skate. Many other kids, most likely at the prompting of their parents, would slush around on the wet surface, creating soaking wet snow pants, weighted down coats and knitted mittens that resembled wet sponges. My sister, Jackie, and I would go home sweaty and dripping wet from our afternoon of "skating." We were told to go in the side door of the house and throw all our wet clothes down the stairs to the basement where my mom would sort and dry them.

If the weather wasn't creating a slushy surface and the ice was hard, we could venture to the ice ramp, one of the exciting features of the Crandall Park rink, that went from the old clubhouse down to the ice rink. The 20-foot-long ramp was intimidating and downright scary, with ruts worn into the grooved surface and some bumps that resembled small frozen rolling waves, making it difficult to navigate for anyone, regardless of skating ability. Actually, the decline was hardly noticeable when covered with grass in the summer months. A record player, with a heavy-duty microphone propped up by the speaker and manned by a teenager in the clubhouse, blasted "skating music" from the large metal speakers that hung from wooden poles placed around the rink. Although typical music from the Sixties was played, like the Monkees and the Fifth Dimension, it seemed to matter more to the girls than the boys what songs were playing.

Another attraction at Crandall Park was the sledding hill next to the clubhouse. Jackie and I rarely had the option of sliding on the hill since we wore our ice skates from home to the rink and couldn't change into boots. Kids would slide down the hill on plastic saucers that the Park loaned out, while we watched in envy, yearning to give our weary ankles a rest. Jackie and I would always hear our friends on the sliding hill bragging about how much fun they were having. We gradually came to realize they were afraid to ice skate and the sliding hill wasn't quite so daunting. Besides, we would often go to the "real" sledding hills at the Glens Falls Country Club, which were for the more serious sledders—like Jackie and myself.

Even with the leather straps tightly wound around my ankles, my dad would often look at me bewildered as to why my ankles would still sag to the ice. I would try and skate down the ice ramp only to be clenching the wooden railing that was on the side of the ramp, fearful of being run over by the more aggressive skaters, as my ankles wobbled and my skates headed in opposite directions. One day, thinking he would encourage me, he took me to the ice ramp and held me by my armpits as we slid down the ramp, navigating our way through the ruts and grooves while gaining speed. For the first time, the ramp was fun. When we tried it a second time, an older man wearing a red flannel shirt, green wool pants, pack boots and a navigator-style cap with the flaps over his ears and dark eyebrows, came trudging out of the clubhouse and, embarrassingly, scolded my dad for taking me down the ice ramp. "Jerry, you should know better than that! If you slipped the boy would be injured."

My dad, embarrassed and evidently having dealt with the guy before, called him "Apple Head" as we skated off. Anytime I spotted this man at the park after that, I shied away from him thinking he would take vengeance on me. Several years later, when I was in junior high school and was cutting through the park with a friend, that same man shouted at us to move on. My friend said, "That's Apple Head!" Apparently "Apple Head" was his unofficial nickname. I later learned he was the official city-appointed 'over-seer' of the park. I wondered if he remembered me from the ramp incident.

After I had advanced to single blade skates, the double runner skates were handed down to my younger brother, Steven. Although he had stronger ankles, he went through the similar routine of learning to skate. Steven didn't have much time on the double runner ice skates since Peter, the third in line and only a year younger than Steven, needed use of the skates. When my youngest brother, Joe, finally inherited the worn-out double runner skates, some of the eyelets for the laces were missing and the leather was scuffed and thin. Poor little Joey was pushed around the rink, in his snow suit, and double runner skates with dull blades, by his four older siblings.

Because of all the attention Joe got as the baby of the family, he learned to skate quicker than the others and quickly tossed the double runners into the basement and moved on to the single blade skates. By this time, my mom had started skating with us when she was not worn out from outfitting five kids with winter clothes and skates. She would join in on our games of tag, but she shied away from the ramp.

When I was in fifth grade, I received a brand-new pair of black leather hockey skates for Christmas. The new skates encouraged me to venture over to the hockey rink at Crandall Park. I would wait until the guys playing hockey left the rink and then skate around, crashing into the four-foot-high boards, pretending I was being "checked into the boards" like Bobby Orr or Phil Esposito.

Coming from a family of hockey enthusiasts, my dad had several hockey sticks stored in the basement. He sawed ten inches off the handle of one of the sticks so it would fit my height. I quickly discovered that wrapping the blade and handle in electrical tape made the stick look more official, like the professionals I saw on our black and white television.

Electrical tape became an obsession to me. I would wrap the four hockey sticks we had with the tape, then re-wrap them in a different pattern. After using all the electrical tape I could find in my dad's workshop, I would ask my friends to bring me electrical tape. My dad started purchasing it in three packs. I guess he figured I could have worse habits than being fixated on electrical tape. My younger brothers joined me in taping stick blades and handles.

After saving up my money from birthday cards and doing chores, I was able to purchase a new hockey stick with a curved blade as opposed to the straight blades on our other sticks. That stick got wrapped in electrical tape as well. I had assumed that the curved blade would give my slap shot an added boost of power. Apparently it did as one of my neighborhood friends went home crying after getting hit in the face with the puck.

The street in front of our house quickly became a destination point for neighborhood kids to play street hockey. It didn't matter what the weather conditions were because we usually played in our rubber pack boots and some kids showed up in sneakers even in freezing temperatures. We would set up goals, using scrap pieces of wood, car mats or anything we could find that wouldn't blow away. Of course, we had to kick the goals to the side of the street if a car or snowplow came by. There were usually enough kids showing up with hockey sticks to form three- or four-person teams. I was the only kid with a wide blade goalie stick, so I often got drafted to be goalie.

Since the Debrule family lived only a block away, they saw all the activity and several of the Debrule boys started playing as well. They had the idea of moving the games to the alley between Kenworthy Avenue and Stoddard Avenue. The alley surface proved to be far superior to the street surface that the city trucks often plowed and sanded. We could get off some excellent fast-moving slap shots in the alley that we couldn't in the salted and sanded street.

One day we were engaged in an intense game when a city plow truck slowly turned into the alley and began spreading sand all across our hockey rink. The Debrule boys were in such dismay that they began yelling at the plow driver, using some words I was not familiar with at the time. They then grabbed shovels and started scraping the sand off the road surface. I went home to get our family snow shovel to join in, but just as I leaped off my front porch with my shovel in hand, a Glens Falls Police patrol car turned down the alley from Stoddard Street. Everyone scattered home, not wanting to explain to their parents why the police were involved. Later, we tried playing hockey on the sand-covered alley but it just didn't work as the puck wouldn't slide in the sand. We gave up on the alley rink.

Since we now had five kids on ice skates, the following winter my dad decided to build an ice rink in our backyard, complete with a homemade hockey net made out of wood and chicken wire fencing. Not to be outdone by "Apple Head," he even built a ramp for us to skate down. Any night that was cold enough for the rink to freeze over, my dad would go out in the backyard and flood the rink with water from our hose. Since the hose would freeze as well, he always brought matches with him to un-thaw the water spigot. The rink was a great idea but, as hard as he tried, my dad could not create an ice surface suitable for skating—even for us beginners. Pine needles would continually drop onto the ice causing us kids to stumble and our yard was too small to play hockey. The most entertainment we kids got from the backyard ice rink was whipping my younger brothers around on a sled on the ice until they wiped out, which brought on crying and my mother popping out the back door to investigate.

In 1968 my grandparents were forced to move from their home on Lawrence Street in Glens Falls because of urban renewal and the Eminent Domain Act, which was used to obtain land for a company called Kaymr. Since they were having a house built in Queensbury, they temporarily moved to the Trout Pavilion Hotel on Kattskill Bay in Lake George. My grandmother was friends with the Palmer family who owned the hotel and lived in a nearby house. She would work as a chambermaid at the hotel during the summer months as well as babysit the Palmer's children. Going to visit my grandparents was fascinating for all us kids. Since it was off-season for the hotel, we had free access to all the rooms. My sister, my cousins and I would play hide and seek throughout the historic hotel that Shirley Temple, as well as gangsters Al Capone and Jack "Legs" Diamond, had stayed at 40 years prior. We even found the candy counter to be unlocked with free access. My grandparents set up a Christmas tree in the grand main room overlooking the lake, which added to the fascination.

My dad, my uncles and my Aunt Judy shoveled off a section of Lake George in front of the hotel to make a hockey rink. They strategically placed boards on each end of the shoveled of area to make goals for the rink. It was a great rink except that whenever an errant shot would go wide of the net, the puck would be lost in the snow, sometimes to be dug out or sometimes to be lost, somewhere on the lake. After running out of pucks, everyone just skated around. Unfortunately, with the ever-changing weather on Lake George in the winter, it became impractical to keep shoveling off the snow to skate. My grandparents moved out of the Trout Pavilion the next year and into their newly built home in Queensbury. The Palmer family sold the hotel and, sadly, several years later, the historic Trout Pavilion burnt to the ground allegedly due to faulty wiring.

Hovey Pond is a small pond on the outskirts of Glens Falls that now has a walk-around trail and benches. In the early nineteen hundreds, the clay bottom was used for making bricks, but by the 1970s it was just an ignored pond by the side of the road nestled across from neighboring homes. My uncles and my Aunt Judy occasionally skated on Hovey Pond and suggested we shovel it off to play hockey. We soon started clearing off the ice to play hockey until my Uncle Mack, who always knew someone who owned whatever he needed, showed up with a snowblower to clear off the ice. The snowblower was working great until it got jammed up with slushy snow.

Mack was experienced in dealing with faulty equipment (mostly motorcycles) and knew to turn off the snowblower before clearing it out, but he didn't realize that once he cleared the slushy jam with his fingers, the stored-up energy would propel the blades on the snowblower. He promptly had the top of his middle finger cut off. I recall sitting in the back seat of my dad's car watching Mack hold his hand above his head to slow the bleeding as we rushed him to the hospital. We never did get in our hockey game that day and that was the last time we skated at Hovey Pond. Mack had a shortened middle finger the rest of his life and he wore his scar like a medal. He would proudly explain the story of his lost finger to anyone who inquired.

I often spent vacation time in Chilson, New York, where my Uncle Bruce worked as a forest ranger. My cousin, Jeff, and I would play hockey on the frozen swamps behind his house near Putt's Pond. This required little to no shoveling, no snowblowers and no interruption from passing cars or snowplows. There were a few local kids who joined in with my sister and cousins in skating around the marshes as well as Jeff's black lab dog chasing us as we tried to skate away from him. We engaged in a few hockey games but without snowbanks or curbs or four-foot-high boards, an errant shot would go skimming across the frozen marsh for yards and yards causing a delay each time as we retrieved the puck. The reeds sticking up from the frozen marsh were also obstacles as we would trip over them with our skates.

It was fun being out in the brisk air and on clear ice, but I preferred the street hockey games back home where cross-checking and elbows were as expected as the snow plow spreading sand; and at Crandall Park with the rutted ramp and the rock music playing. Little brother Joe, being 12 years younger than I, had the benefit of a new enclosed skating rink on Fire Road in Glens Falls, that was constructed well after I had moved away. Having exposure to an enclosed skating rink and with the introduction of Youth Hockey in Glens Falls, Joe went on to play for the Glens Falls High School hockey team that won the New York State High School Championship in 1990. He never gave our family the credit for our "learn to skate or else" approach when he was a toddler but, he was (and still is at 49) a good skater. I was at that game, in Utica, playing vicariously through my little brother, as if I was in the alley back home, playing against the Debrule brothers with my curved stick wrapped in electrical tape and scoring the winning goal with a slap shot into the homemade chicken wire net. Joe was playing for two generations of "wannabe" hockey stars.

Crandall Park Ice Rink, 1970

The Summer of 1973

Someone once said: "It ain't easy being a teenager." Millions of people have most likely cited that quote. On June 6, 1973, I became a teenager and, rightly, began to partake in teenage activities. Most of the "activities" were parent-sanctioned and I took great advantage of the recreational opportunities our area had to offer. Gallivanting around the Lake George area as well as in the city of Glens Falls produced many memorable summers, including the summer of 1973.

The Watergate investigation was front and center in the national news, which would have meant nothing to me as a teenager except that one of the major conspirators in the break-in of the Democrat Headquarters in Washington, D.C. was John W. Dean. The librarian at Crandall Library would look at me over the top of her bifocals when I checked out a book, asking, "Oh, do you know you have a famous name?"

When school began that fall, I got to my 8th grade Social Studies class and the teacher, Mr. Harrington, would grill me with Watergate questions (I'm not sure, but he may have been a Democrat). My friends, who could have cared less who the President was, would joke with me about being on TV and asking, "Are you related to that guy?" So, I got used to it. I am still used to it since once or twice year someone will mention my name and its correlation to the Watergate scandal. My reply is: "Do you know how old you must be to remember that?"

It was our family tradition to head to the Adirondacks the

first day that school ended for summer vacation. During the last week of school, we would begin to prepare for our trip by digging out our sleeping bags from the storage area in back of our home and airing them out on the clothes line that was strung from our back porch. There was no mistaking our big blue tent with white stripes on the roof. That made it easy to spot whether folded up in storage or set up on the campground. We dug that out as well, along with the tent poles, cots, and our metal Coleman cooler with the dent in the side. No one ever owned up to putting the dent in the cooler, so we just assumed my dad bought it that way.

Each of us kids packed our treasures to keep us entertained when it rained, which was often. My preference was baseball cards and fishing tackle. I could sit in the tent and read baseball cards for hours when it rained. I could not say as much about the fishing pole. I was frequently fishing but rarely catching anything.

As the children in our family grew, we evolved from local campgrounds, to which we could pretty much commute from home, to camping with relatives at Lake Eaton and Putts Pond. In the summer of 1973, we had a one-year old baby, my brother Joseph, join us. Many neighbors and friends questioned taking five kids, including the one-year old baby, camping in the Adirondacks. We did it anyway, mostly out of lack of funds to stay at a resort. We opted to go to Putts Pond for the week since my Aunt Ginny and Uncle Bruce lived up the road from the campground. If there were any "misfortunes" with any of the young children, my aunt and uncle would be close by. In the early 1970s there was no State Campground Reservation System. It was first come, first served. The closer to July 4th the camper arrived, the less likely he was going to get a good site, or any site at all. For some reason, we got off to a late start that year and didn't get to Putts Pond until Monday, two days before July 4th. We were directed to go to the "overflow" area of the campground. This was uncharted territory for our family. The overflow area was a graded sandy area with no listed sites, just a "put it anywhere" area. So that is what we did. We set up our tent and dining canopy towards the edge of the sandy area next to an unattended camping trailer. It wasn't until the next day that the folks who owned the trailer showed up and turned out to be friends of ours from church, the Howe family.

Other than dealing with massive amounts of black flies and mosquitoes from the swamp next to the overflow area, we had an uneventful week and the summer got off to a good start—baby and all. We decided to go back to Putts Pond at the end of August and get a better campsite. My dad taught biology and chemistry in summer school every year and that would limit our camping to days before the fourth of July. We were determined to get our camping in regardless of summer school. In the middle of July, we set up camp at Moreau Lake, only 20 minutes from where my dad was teaching. He would get up in the morning, head to school and then after school stop home to feed the cats and collect the mail and be back at the campground by early afternoon. On some days he would even carpool with another teacher who had the same idea.

Fortunately, he was carpooling the day we experienced such a violent storm that the tent started collapsing. My mother finally hit her breaking point and loaded all the kids, including baby Joey, into the car and drove home. The next day my dad went back and broke camp. He set the tent up in the back yard to dry out, but none of us kids wanted to sleep in our backyard. It just wasn't the same as being in the woods.

The summer of 1973 was also the year of "Robert Garrow," the murdering mad man from Syracuse. Garrow had killed a young girl in Syracuse and then fled to the Adirondacks where he killed four more people. The manhunt for Garrow started on July 14 and was focused in Hamilton County. Unlike Watergate and Vietnam, the manhunt was talked about daily by everyone—especially teenagers, since he had killed a teenager. A State Police investigator even went to Hudson Falls High School, where my dad was teaching summer school, to question a teacher whose last name was Garrow. Many people changed their vacation plans, but some didn't take it seriously until Garrow tried kidnapping a young girl at the Word of Life Camp in Schroon Lake. Being that Garrow was from Mineville, New York, which is the next town over from Chilson and Putts Pond, we decided not to head back up to Putts Pond a second time that summer. It didn't help that the hit movie for that summer was *Deliverance* starring Burt Reynolds fending off backwoods maniacs—maniacs like Robert Garrow. Garrow was eventually caught near his sister's home in Mineville after a 12-day manhunt. My Uncle Bruce was one of the Rangers that cornered him.

As a side note, forty-two years later, we were at our camp in Parishville, just inside the Adirondack Park, when two convicts, David Sweat and Richard Matt, escaped from Dannemora Prison, and another manhunt took place in the Adirondacks. It was thought that the convicts were breaking into hunting camps and taking back roads through the Park. Some of our camp neighbors, and my wife, Terri, debated on whether they would venture as far as our campground. It was decided that since most of the campers in our area of the Adirondacks were so heavily armed, it would have been stupid for the prisoners to come our way. Matt was shot and killed by police and Sweat was captured on June 28, 2015 near Malone, New York, 45 miles from our camp. It was not really a "close call," but even the Governor admitted at one point in the manhunt that he had no idea where they could be.

After the Garrow scare we did several camping trips to Fourth Lake. "Fourth Lake" is a very open-ended description of a campground. There are at least four Fourth Lakes that I have been to in the Adirondacks and more than one official state campground with that name. The Fourth Lake we camped at was across the road from Lake Luzerne and Hadley Mountain. The water quality there was superior to that at Moreau Lake and we were still within commuting distance of Hudson Fall High School. We set up our campsite, complete with a baby crib, clothesline and sand toys scattered about. Although the Garrow incident made everyone think more and was certainly the chatter around campfires, we felt safe at Fourth Lake and camped and picnicked there numerous times during the Seventies.

Our neighbors across the street, the Castellucci's, had a camp on Lake Champlain and, since I was now a teenager, I was permitted to spend a week at their camp away from my family. I packed my bicycle, my suitcase, my snorkel and fins and my fishing pole and away I went. Between my neighbor friends, Greg and Val, and their cousins, we caught all kinds of fish ranging from perch to bass to sheepshead. It was the most productive week of fishing I had ever experienced. Of course, back in 1973, there was little talk of mercury in the fish or of limiting how many you ate, so we cleaned perch and fried them up every night but one.

Then we thought that one night we would make pizza. We talked throughout the day about making our deluxe pizza that night and sitting by the lake chomping down our delicacy. As we pulled the hot pizza out of the oven it drew the attention of Greg's younger siblings and a few of the cousins. Greg and I decided we weren't about to share our pizza, so Greg cleverly soaked the pizza with hot sauce. One bite and the younger kids went running off screaming that their tongues were on fire.

Greg's mother showed up and decided the proper punishment for Greg and me was to eat the entire pizza while she watched. That we gladly did, because (when Greg saw her marching towards the camp) he scraped off as much hot sauce as he could. Other than having his mom watch us eat, we enjoyed our delicious pizza.

The next day as we climbed Poke-A-Moonshine Mountain our stomachs started acting up, but we trudged on, keeping our distance from the other hikers. We went back to frying perch on our campfire at the beach the next night. As I headed for home at the end of the week, Greg's mom only had one thing to say to me, "John, you're silent but deadly."

I was invited back, so I couldn't have been too troublesome or "deadly" in her terms. It was always great fun to spend time at their camp on Lake Champlain. The summer of 1973 was indeed one of the most eventful of my teenage years and it is certainly one that I am reminded of most often, thanks to Watergate, Richard Nixon's famous line, "I am not a crook," and a politician with my name.

A family camping trip to Putts Pond.
I hope the crib was brought inside the tent at night.

Boy Scouts

Glens Falls, New York's Boy Scout Troop One was appropriately named, because it was one of the first Scout troops to be established in the city around 1915 with my grandfather being one of its founding members of the troop. When I joined that same Troop One, after completing my Cub Scout years, we met in the basement of the Baptist Church on Maple Street. I'm not sure if that was the original meeting place for Troop One, but the equipment that was inherited appeared to be from that era: musty old canvass tents and tarps with weathered wooden tent poles, army surplus shovels, a mishmash of metal tent stakes and ropes that smelled of kerosene were stuffed into a storage room that was adjacent to our meeting room.

We met in a spacious, gray-painted, stale-smelling room that was directly under the sanctuary of the church. Old wooden chairs and a large maple desk with a few missing drawers circled around a freestanding chalkboard made for our official Monday night meeting spot. An old dartboard that hung on the wall, and the darts that had wooden grips and rusty steel tips, got used more than our Scout handbooks.

Scout Troop One had been non-existent for several years during the 1960s and early 1970s. In fact, no one at the church could recall the last time a Scout troop had met there. A few men in the leadership at the Baptist Church thought it would be good for the church and the community to get the troop active again since there were boys in the church that obviously needed direction in their lives and the accountability that scouting would bring. It was decided by the church leaders that a stern, well-disciplined leader was needed to lead Troop One, so they formed a committee to come up with a leader.

Somehow my Uncle Mack got nominated for the role. Mack was the most unlikely of candidates being that he didn't go to church, he didn't have any children, he smoked a couple of packs of cigarettes a day, he was a part-time bartender, a part-time carpenter, a substitute schoolteacher, a steamboat captain and he led a lifestyle that was secretly the envy of the curmudgeon leaders in the church.

Uncle Mack was often very elusive, sometimes not being heard from for several days, and difficult to reach back in the days of rotary telephones. It was that precise "jet setting" lifestyle of his that attracted teenage boys to join the troop. Other troops had gray-haired, bespectacled, pipe-smoking leaders, with bellies that hung over their uniform belts and an aftershave odor about them; we had James Bond, Agent 007. Being under Uncle Mack's tutelage was cool and intriguing to young men looking to make their impression on the world and, since most of us were initially "directed" by our parents to join the scouts, it made our meeting time much more pleasurable to attend.

Although Mack took the position very seriously by having us stand at attention, memorize the scout pledge and show respect, he couldn't hide his boyish enthusiasm and carefree approach to life. Our Monday night meetings sometimes started at 7:00 pm, and sometimes started at 7:30 pm or later, whenever Mack arrived to unlock the doors to the church and let us in. Initially it was very aggravating to wait for Mack to arrive each week and then it became amusing. Many times, it was just "car trouble" that caused his tardiness. We got used to "Mack time" when it came to meetings and hikes. Arriving in the parking lot with his car tires squealing and the radio blaring, Mack always had a legitimate reason for being late. The scouts grew accustomed to his stories about stopping to assist someone with a flat tire or dropping off a friend at a remote location or having an important meeting to attend—even though his primary jobs were in construction and bartending Mack knew a lot of people and they were all very fond of him—most spoke favorably of Mack and chuckled about his lifestyle.

During our tenure with Mack as our scout leader, he was married and divorced but never had children. The boys in the troop became Mack's surrogate kids—ideal for him in that he only had to spend a couple of hours on Monday nights in a teaching mode and a couple of weekends a month camping and hiking. He never had to deal with report cards or household chores or even an illness. If you were sick on a scout night you stayed home, and Mack never broached the subject of report cards, even though he had a teaching degree and sometimes filled in as a substitute shop teacher.

Initially, there were a few bumps in the road as Mack tried to work within the boundaries of the whole Boy Scout structure of mottos, merit badges and accountability. Our meetings were organized in that Mack took attendance and we said the motto each week and, occasionally, worked on merit badges and played some games, but mostly we planned our camping trips and hikes of which there were many. Mack even traded in his Datsun 240Z sportscar for a used Ford station wagon to haul us boys and camping gear. At our peak, there were 20 boys in the troop from several area schools. Occasionally, one of the scout's fathers or a fellow bartender would assist at a meeting or join on a hike but primarily it was just Mack and his boys. Our hiking destinations often discouraged the "unfit" from joining in, which was fine with us.

Whether it was to appease the church elders, or it was truly meant to enrich the Boy Scout experience, one Monday night Mack invited the men who had selected him as Scout Leader to participate in a meeting. We were used to seeing these elders snappily dressed in black or brown suits on Sunday mornings, so when they showed up at our meeting in flannel shirts and hiking boots it roused our curiosity. They stoically observed us from the back of the room as we stood at attention and did the Pledge of Allegiance and the Boy Scout motto. As the meeting progressed, the elders loosened up and actually had a good time interacting with us scouts. They taught us new knots along with stories of when they had to use them, as well as sharing experiences of being in the woods, which we were all about. That evening turned out to be a blessing for everyone as it gave Mack more confidence as the "leader" to participate in more official Boy Scout sanctioned functions.

The first function to which we were invited to by the local Council was the Klondike Derby. This was a mid-winter event in which each troop built a dog sled that the scouts would pull around in the snowy woods, stopping at various stations to build a fire from flint and steel, perform a first aid function or complete some other scout task. After we agreed as a troop to attend the Derby, Mack showed up the next Monday night with his power tools, a stockpile of wood and a pair of snow skis. We proceeded to build an incredible dog sled that, quite honestly, could have been used by real Eskimos and sled dogs.

When we arrived at the Klondike Derby, all the other troops, with their troop-built sleds, were in awe of our sled. We were a very diverse group of scouts without the uniforms and modern gear that many of the other troops sported, but at that event we were the talk of the town. One of our troop members, Don Middleton, was born without legs and had two prosthetic legs. He wore sneakers to the event and, without thinking, Mack blurted out, "Your feet are going to get cold." Don, while wanting to reply, simply said nothing. One of the less bright kids in our troop commented to Mack that Don had "wooden feet." Don did well at the event, trudging through the snow and at one point we had Don sit in the sled while we guided him down the trail. We didn't win any official Scout Council awards that day, but we went home knowing we took the prize for best sled and best sled team.

The Klondike Derby opened the door for us to embark on numerous winter camping trips. We started out going to Camp Wakpominee on the east side of Lake George for an overnight in its very rustic cabins. The temperature dropped so low that night that the Ranger for the camp drove out to the campsite in his beat-up Jeep to check on us—only to find us all huddled in Mack's station wagon with the heat blasting. The Ranger, Mr. Bogart, had us come to his house just a few miles from the camp for hot chocolate and to warm up by his fireplace.

Back at the church basement the following Monday night, we discussed our mistakes, like taking summer-weight sleeping bags, and learned to prepare more for our next winter outing. We took some day hikes in the winter months to Buck Mountain and Tongue Mountain since some of the boys had never hiked in the winter and some of the parents were nervous after the scout camp excursion.

So nervous were the parents that when we went camping at Lake George the following winter one of the fathers, Mr. Stewart, brought along his heated 20-foot camper. Of course, we boys had to sleep in the canvas tents on the crusty snow in our sleeping bags while Mack and Mr. Stewart slept in the camper. We huddled around our campfire cooking hot dogs on a stick and drinking lots of hot chocolate while wondering what exciting things Mack had in store for us the next day. As we awoke in our frozen tents the next morning, reeking of campfire smoke and starving for some type of food other than Pop-Tarts, we were appalled at what happened next. Mack, who had slept in Mr. Stewart's camper all night, had left the campground before we got up, leaving Mr. Stewart to oversee our morning activities which were . . . none. As we stood around yet another smoldering campfire, Mack pulled up to the campsite in his station wagon.

We were hoping Mack had gone out to get us breakfast, but were we ever wrong. Several girls in their late teens or early 20s stepped out of his station wagon, dressed in nice winter coats and designer boots with glimmering scarfs draped around their necks. They were smiling and giggling—at us boys! Unbeknownst to us, Mack was the official chairman of the Lake George Winter Carnival that year and one of his responsibilities was to crown the Winter Carnival Snow Queen. He had to bring the contestants to several events and observe their charming personalities to determine a winner. The interaction he observed from our group only proved he had made a huge mistake. Fourteen-year-old boys, smelling like smoke, with dirty hair and having used the woods as a rest room, did not present a good social interaction for a potential Snow Queen. We began kicking the crusty snow with our pack boots and frozen toes and scouted around for sticks and branches to throw into the fire, not knowing what to say to anyone, including Mack, who had just broken a sacred vow by bringing girls to a Boy Scout function.

After quickly realizing the gross error of judgment he had made, Mack packed the ladies back into his station wagon and returned them from whence they came. He tried to salvage our outing by taking us to the end of the lake to participate in the snow sculpture building contest. Since it was 12 degrees outside, the snow could not be sculpted, so we did some more standing around kicking the crusty snow. Once back at the church and dispersing to go home, we boys agreed that this trip was a bust. Mack had some making up to do.

"What the hell were you guys thinking?" Mack shouted at us in front of the Glens Falls Police Sargent. Earlier in the day, we had taken a 16-mile bicycle ride from the church to the Boy Scout Camp. Once at the camp we ate our packed lunches, finished the water from our canteens, climbed back onto our bicycles and headed towards the church. This was all done to fulfill the requirements for a merit badge. Since we had several levels of bike riders, some with ten speeds, some with no speeds, and some with short legs (or no legs), Mack thought it best that he drive his station wagon instead of riding a bike himself so he could better monitor our progress or attend to a flat tire. At least that is what his rationale was to us boys. We assessed that another reason was so he could smoke cigarettes throughout the day while cruising in his car. On regular hikes he would occasionally "light up" while on a trail and we thought nothing of it as it made us appear to be more like "rugged" mountain men.

When we trekked back to the church, the more aggressive boys made it back well in front of a few who were lagging behind. Mack hung back with his car keeping an eye on the slower peddlers assuming we were safe back at the church. Being teenage boys without supervision, we started entertaining ourselves by pretending we were breaking into the locked church. We started climbing up the brick ledges and acting as if we were prying open the windows. It was all in fun until someone in the neighborhood called the police. The police Sargent arrived seconds before Mack pulled into the parking lot, both converging on us boys at the same time. The late-arriving scouts slowly peddled into the parking lot with grins on their faces, happy that the showboating bikers with their fancy ten speed bikes had gotten into trouble—with the law, no less.

After Mack cleared things up with the police, we were "released" from our event to go home. It was a quiet meeting the following Monday night.

Our next official BSA (Boy Scouts of America) event was a local council jamboree in which each troop was to bring plaster casts of animal footprints that they had observed on a troop hike. It was assumed that most troops would have deer hooves, raccoon and squirrel prints and maybe a coyote or possibly even a bear paw cast. Mack, not to be outdone by the politically correct leaders, had a better idea. All Mack needed was a little cooperation from some rebellious teens and he could pull it off. We were all in.

Mack had more connections with people than anyone I ever knew. He knew people in all professions in every state. One of his "buddies" owned a game farm on the outskirts of Lake George and, allegedly, he gave us permission to go to the farm and make plaster casts of ostriches, elk, antelope and buffalo. We would show those other scouts who had the coolest troop. As the two cars hauling scouts were driving down a back-country road, which soon turned into a dirt road, I wondered out loud why the game farm wasn't a more "formal" place—like the Animal Forest Kingdom in York Beach, Maine, which had a big sign over the road and warning signs to not feed the animals.

As we pulled up to a muddy turnaround area where heavy brush that grew along a chain link fence had been cleared, I was sure it was a case of bad directions. Then Mack parked his station wagon and said, "I think this is it," while perusing the landscape looking for any other "witnesses." We walked a short distance through the wooded area until coming upon a metal gate with a chain and heavy-duty lock on it. *Why isn't the owner there to meet us? Where are the animals? Where is the snack shack?* These were a few of my thoughts. It all seemed very shady, even to teenage boys. Mack pointed out the ostriches and the buffalo on the far corner of the property, a few hundred yards away, grazing in the field and minding their own business like we should have been doing. Mack then said, "Quick, get out that plaster and the molds and crawl under that gate."

We did as we were instructed, three boys mixing the plaster and pouring it into some muddy hoof prints with the rest of us standing guard, presumably to hold off any charging animals. Since it took 20 minutes or so for the plaster to harden enough for transport, Mack thought it best that we wait on the other side of the fence. We crawled back under the gate. Peering through the fence, I was wondering if the animals would charge at us or, worse yet, if the owner of the animals would show up. Mack sent a couple of the older scouts back under the gate to collect the plaster casts while the rest of us, including Mack, nervously clung to the chain link fence.

Once back at the church we cleaned up our casts and labeled them for the jamboree. At the event, every other troop, unaware of our shady adventure, just passed by our table of plaster casts disinterested in what we had accomplished. It may not have gotten the results we wanted—recognition from other troops—but the experience tightened the bond of the boys in the troop.

Berry Mill Pond is a decent size pond setting next to Grizzle Ocean, a three-mile hike from Putts Pond near Ticonderoga. Berry Mill Pond became our home away from home. Even though our scout troop hiked Tongue Mountain and Buck Mountain numerous times, we camped at Berry Mill Pond a dozen times over the years. We knew the trail so well we would sometimes go in at night, although a couple of parents with-held their boys from going on those hikes, deeming them too dangerous. Since there were three lean-tos surrounding the pond, after hiking in we never worried about setting up camp. Once established, we would gather firewood, fish and play epic three-hour long games of capture the flag in the surrounding woods. One trip we stumbled upon a metal john boat hidden in the underbrush near the pond. A few of us paddled over to Grizzle Ocean to fish for the day.

Another time at Berry Mill Pond, we all experienced some-thing we had never seen before. We had arrived on a Friday evening in early April and the pond was still covered in ice. The next day was unseasonably warm and sunny and in mid-afternoon a slight breeze came blowing in from the east and literally blew the "needles" of melting ice off the pond and over the waterfall by the lean-to.

That afternoon we caught numerous Great Northern Pike by the dam after the ice went out. Although we almost always left for our hikes on Friday afternoons after school, one week-end we didn't get started until Saturday morning. When we pulled into the parking lot at Putt's Pond, we noticed another vehicle parked at the trail head for Berry Mill Pond, which was unusual since we rarely encountered anyone on our hikes there. Knowing that there were three lean-tos there, we were confident we would be able to set up our camp.

When we arrived at our favorite lean-to, there were two guys in camouflage outfits with camouflage paint on their faces, taking target practice at tin cans lined up along the pond. Proudly flashing their rifles, they grinned at us scouts as we came up the crest of the trail approaching the lean-to. We froze in our tracks not knowing what to do. Even Mack was taken by surprise, which made me nervous, since nothing ever rattled Mack except us boys.

Mack made a gesture to the two camouflaged gunslingers as if to say, "We didn't see a thing," and told us to turn around and head back to the car. I commented to Mack that we could go to one of the other shelters and set up camp, to which Mack stoically replied, "Just head to the car." He was having no part in exposing his boys to stray bullets or red-neck shenanigans. I spent a week at the Boy Scout Camp the following summer earning some merit badges and because of the abundance of hiking and camping trips orchestrated by Mack, I was able to achieve the Life Badge, a couple of levels from Eagle scout. Ranks were never really significant to any of us in Troop One. The life experiences we gained from Mack's tutelage far exceeded doing the book work required for badges.

Mack started a new job and handed over the leadership of the troop to Mr. Glenn, who assisted on and off over the years. Most of us boys were now approaching 16 years old and other interests took up our time. Mr. Glenn tried to make a go of the troop for a short time, but no one was going to fill Mack's shoes and the troop eventually folded.

What Mack accomplished in the lives of a dozen boys over several years cannot be easily measured and surely not duplicated. Sadly, Mack died of a massive heart attack at age 61 in 2003.

Uncle Mack, at right, and the Boy Scouts

Slippery Slopes

My bedroom in our house in Glens Falls was situated in such a way that when I laid in bed at night, I could gaze out the window at the lighted ski trails on West Mountain. Often mesmerized by the lights brightening up the sky over the mountain, I would drift off to sleep wondering what it would be like to ski under those lights. Having never attempted downhill skiing, I was convinced I was forever left to the mundane cross-country skiing that I had dabbled in for several years. Cross country skiing was relatively inexpensive, and I could do it at Crandall Park with minimal snow and no supervision. But a few of my friends boasted of their exploits at slalom skiing and I did so much desire to be a part of the club.

As I expressed my desire to take up downhill skiing to my Uncle Allan, he excitedly assured me that he was an excellent instructor and he could teach me how to ski. He was proud that he had taught his four daughters how to ski and looked forward to having another successful graduate of the "Dean School of Skiing." Uncle Allan was on the ski patrol which, in my eyes, made him an expert. He rounded up some well-used skis, ski poles and a pair of ski boots with some malfunctioning metal buckles that may have been slightly safer than the funky outdated bindings that often popped off even when standing still. Although it wasn't fancy equipment, it was functional, and it got me onto the slopes.

Standing at the base of the mountain, I was intimidated by

the steep trails and the hustle and bustle of skiers coming and going. Since I had all the right equipment and was with my cousins, I felt a sense of belonging. That feeling quickly disappeared when I grabbed hold of the rope tow at the Hickory Hill ski area. As the rope slid quickly through my ski gloves, I felt a quick tug and off went my glove, somehow attached to the rope.

Not sure as to how to keep my balance while holding onto my ski poles, I ended up taking off my skis and walking up the first incline to the top of the lift to retrieve my glove. It occurred to me that the rope tow was the most basic "lift" on the mountain, as I had observed little kids, who were barely able to reach the rope, quickly grab hold and be propelled up the hill. My cousins encouraged me by stating they had a difficult time with the rope as well, but I didn't believe them.

Hickory Hill was a family-operated ski center in Warrensburg. Numerous families were the stockholders and each family participated in the operation of the "resort" which consisted of a rope tow, several poma lifts, a steel-sided lodge with a fire pit, rest rooms and a snack bar. Poma lifts essentially consist of a pole with an attached small disc that fits under your butt and pulls you up the mountain. Uncle Allan and his family had skied at Hickory Hill for several years and my cousins had all learned to ski there. I didn't understand how the entire stockholder thing worked, but Uncle Allan seemed to do his fair share of manning lifts and patrolling the mountain.

Usually a tolerant man, teaching me to ski really tested his patience. He was insistent that his method of teaching the snowplow worked flawlessly when he had taught his four daughters and their friends how to ski. I could sense a level of frustration that I had never seen before when Uncle Allan spotted me sitting in a snowbank, with my ski tips sticking straight up in the air and my poles laying several feet away. At first, he simply encouraged me to keep my center of gravity lower and bend my knees more. A few hours later, after several more "bend your knees more" and "this isn't that difficult," he just skied off and left me without saying a word. Never one to get angry, I think he was questioning why his training methods worked so well with others but not with me.

I may have set the Hickory Hill record for falling off the poma lift, if one would consider it "falling off" of a pole that is pulling you up a mountain. If I wasn't losing my balance, then it was my skis crisscrossing or my bindings releasing causing me to do a flop-like landing in the snow. I kept my head down while in the lodge as I had started hearing other skiers complain about someone who kept "shutting the lift down" because of all his miscues on the lift. Even my cousins grew bored with my flailing and flopping and came up with lines like "maybe you should take a break in the lodge" or "maybe you'd do better without us watching you." I sensed it might be better for everyone that I ski on my own.

After a few weekends of not giving up, I was able to snow plow my way from the lodge to the parking lot and back up the rope tow and even the short poma lift. I was soon telling my friends in the high school cafeteria that I was downhill skiing. A couple of kids, well-known in school as expert skiers, skeptically asked me where I was skiing. When I proudly stated it was Hickory Hill, they started laughing out loud while making some statements regarding "a bunny hill," insinuating that I was far from their level. I quickly ascertained that during lunch period I should talk about other things than skiing. The best-kept secret in upstate New York for skiing, at least in the 1970s, was Hickory Hill. While the base trails around the lodge were basic beginner trails, the upper half of the mountain contained numerous steep expert trails and a long ridge trail. Once I was able navigate the poma lift to the top of the mountain, the ridge trail became my favorite destination. It had breathtakingly beautiful views of Warren County as well as long stretches of moderate downhill grades that I could maneuver with my snowplow turns. According to my cousins, Hickory Hill had the fourth steepest trails in New York State. I didn't know if that was factual or their perception, but it sounded legitimate to me. The trails were maintained by the stockholders with a few hired hands to run the grooming "cat." Since the upper trails were so steep, as folks navigated the rocks, they left giant moguls and some exposed boulders that were capable of snapping skis or bruising ankles. With no chair lifts and only a simple lodge, Hickory Hill lacked the glitz and glamor of the New York State-run Ski Centers and the resorts of Vermont. Quite simply, folks preferred to sit in a chair lift or in an enclosed gondola cabin over being pulled by a thin metal pole with a wooden disc seat.

By my second year of skiing, I had mastered the snowplow and was learning to "Stem Cristie," otherwise known as parallel skiing. I got so adept at it that I began to ski the steeper parts of the upper mountain. This time I chose to ski mostly alone so that when I fell or slid down the steep slopes, which I often did, I wasn't embarrassed. From time to time I would catch up with Uncle Allan or my cousins so I could demonstrate my improvements.

One thing about skiing expert trails is that you either improve quickly or you get injured quickly. While skiing at Hickory Hill, I witnessed the ski patrol in action a few times but fortunately, it was never for me. I learned to ski the moguls at the cost of tearing out the metal edges of my skis and popping out of my bindings more times than I can recall. Based upon all the scraping of metal on rock sounds that echoed throughout the trails, I'm sure I wasn't the only one wearing out their skis.

While sitting in the cafeteria in high school, I mustered up the courage to bring up the subject of the difficult trails at

Hickory Hill, remembering the ridicule I received during the prior ski season. Although the ridicule was not as abrasive, I was challenged by the "expert skiers" to join them at West Mountain, which had real trails, and then at Gore Mountain— if I was worthy.

The biggest "I told you so" moment that ever occurred in my high school days happened on a Monday morning at 11:30 a.m. in the cafeteria at Glens Falls High School. I was abruptly greeted by a couple of friends, the "expert" skiers, who stated they had gone to Hickory Hill the day before, "out of default," as it was apparently not their choice. Their exact proclamation was, "Deano, why didn't you tell us about Hickory Hill? That place is bodacious! Those are the biggest moguls we've ever seen." Once the word got out, it soon became a cult following at school to go to Hickory Hill and ski the moguls. Kids who rarely associated with a beginner skier such as myself, began sitting with me at lunch discussing the ins and outs of the trails at "Hickory." I was considered the "go-to" guy for the scoop on Hickory Hill. There was no more talk about a bunny slope. I'm pretty sure the stockholders got a higher return on their investments that year thanks to the skiing junkies from Glens Falls High School.

Once I was accepted as a credible skier, I was asked to join my friends on ski outings to West Mountain, Gore Mountain and, eventually, to Killington Mountain in Vermont. West Mountain was not only visible from my bedroom window, but it was also quite visible from the 6-foot-high windows in the cafeteria of Glens Falls High School. We would sit in the cafeteria looking at the mountain and strategizing how to get there. Only a select few students had access to a car, and there was much politicizing that took place to convince them to drive a group of teens to West Mountain. There were actually a few days when temptation overtook us and, after finding a willing driver, we would leave school after lunch, missing our afternoon classes, and take off to the mountain. However, most days, after classes ended, we would just make a beeline from school to West Mountain and ski on a twilight pass from 3 p.m. to 7 p.m. for $4. If we were fortunate, someone from school would be working the lift and let us ski until the 10:00 p.m. closing time on the $4 pass, conveniently looking the other way as we boarded the chair lift. We skied on ice, on powder, on rocks, in the rain, in the snow, in the bitter cold, it didn't matter, it was an addiction. Working as a stock boy, I saved enough money to purchase new skis, new boots, new poles and, thankfully, new bindings that met the safety guidelines of the ski shop. I even splurged and purchased a sleek-looking baby blue colored ski jacket for $60. After I wore the jacket a few times, my friends began implying that it looked like a girl's jacket. When a couple of girls skied up to me and asked me if it was a girl's jacket, which it wasn't, I was really embarrassed. I went home that night and gave the jacket to my mother.

I ventured off with friends to Gore Mountain, Whiteface Mountain and trekked to Killington many times when I could afford it. Killington cost $28 for a day as opposed to New York State-run centers which were $12, or good old Hickory Hill, which was still a bargain at $8 for a day pass. I pretty much followed the crowd as to where we skied on any given day.

When my schoolmate, Aaron, did a double helicopter off a jump at West Mountain, it was big news, at least in the halls of Glens Falls High School. During that era there were no half pipes or Olympic jumping events other than the high ski jump. Ski equipment was just beginning to be marketed that enabled skiers to do tricks off jumps and do semi-acrobatic stunts. Freestyle ski jumping was at its birthing point. Several high school skiers could do a "helicopter" or a "spread eagle" off make-shift jumps, but it was the reckless jumps off moguls that made the headlines in the cafeteria. Kids would either execute a perfect jump, if only three feet off the ground, or they would catch a tip of their ski and land so awkwardly that their equipment would go flying in several directions on the hard-packed snow, usually with an audience watching.

As we gathered up the scattered poles, goggles and hat for the disheveled skier, we would reassure him that it was a great attempt. It may not have been a great attempt at landing the jump, but it was a great attempt to entertain the dozen or so people watching. Not wanting to miss out on leaving my impression on the group, I would follow along, mimicking the skier in front of me, even doing the wipeout after mistakenly thinking I could pull off the jump. Skiing moguls, jumping and skiing the steepest, triple diamond rated trails, became my passion. There wasn't a jump or steep trail on any mountain that I didn't "attempt" to ski often being egged on by a group of friends whose thoughts of seeing me get injured cryptically entertained them.

In the winter of 1980, as the Olympics took place in Lake Placid, I headed off to Utah to ski the Rockies. After a few years of skiing on ice patches and bare rocks (Hickory Hill), the deep snow and powder of the Rocky Mountains seemed like heaven to ski on.

Most days there was fresh snow and some days a foot of powder, which was brutal on my thigh muscles. On the few days that the trails got worn down or there was rain, I would be one of the only people skiing. The Westerners would complain, "It's way too icy on the trails" to which I would reply, "You don't even know what ice looks like until you've been to Gore Mountain." You could slip on a patch of ice at Gore Mountain that could send you sliding a quarter mile down the side of the mountain.

Not wanting to miss out on any of the triple diamond trails of the West, I took the gondola to the top of Snowbird and then hiked on top of the crusty snow to the top of the mountain. I thought it was cool that a helicopter dropped off some other skiers who had the same thought but had much more money. Although Utah had excellent conditions and challenging trails, I didn't find any trails that matched the uniqueness and "on the brink of death" qualities of New York skiing.

One day after returning to New York, I went back to Gore Mountain, fresh off being spoiled with the Rocky Mountain conditions. Gore was its usual 12 degrees with a wind chill of minus twenty. The skiers that day had their scarves wrapped tightly around their faces to protect themselves from frostbite. I was cruising down the mountain underneath the triple chairlift and spotted a jump at the crest of a drop-off near the chairlift. Not one to shy away from any jump, I hit the jump at cruising speed, dropped my ski tips, spread my legs and brought my ski poles up over my shoulders and did a perfect 'back scratcher.' As I landed on hard packed snow at the base of the jump and skied off, the other skiers on the chairlift began clapping. The adrenaline rush was exhilarating. I had come a long way since the other skiers had complained about the kid who kept shutting down the lift because of his clumsiness.

Shortly before I moved away from Glens Falls and the bedroom with the view of West Mountain, I had the opportunity to ski at West Mountain on New Year's Eve. The protocol at most ski areas was that the ski patrol made their final "sweep" of the mountain after the lifts shut down to make sure everyone was off the mountain before they turned the lights off. That night, I was the last skier to take the lift before closing. When I reached the top of the mountain, I observed thirty or so ski patrollers hanging out and waiting for me to disembark so they could begin their final sweep. I stopped for a moment and looked at the lights over Glens Falls twinkling in the distance, knowing one of those lights was at my childhood home. Contemplating that my time of living in Glens Falls was coming to an end, I reminisced about all the winter nights spent gazing at this very spot from my bedroom window. I slowly skied down to the lodge, stopping a few times at various "lookouts" to take it all in. The ski patrol evidently was taking in the blend of red and green Christmas lights and city glow as well,

Author cross-country skiing

as they creeped down the mountain behind me.

Just as I reached the lodge at the base, the lights went out on the trails, leaving only the lights inside the lodge and a few parking lot lights on. Looking up the mountain just past the "Go-Go" trail and through the shadows of the trees I could see the glow of red torches slithering down the mountain like a slow-moving snake. Each ski patrol member was carrying a red torch and slowly cruising down the dark trails in a zig-zag pattern so that the red flames were creating a large "S" pattern. As I stood there gazing at them as they wended their way to the bottom of the slope, I could only imagine what it looked like from my bedroom window.

Lake George

I learned to swim in the pool at the original YMCA building in downtown Glens Falls. At seven years old I would be dropped off every Saturday morning at the side entrance to the old YMCA, work my way up two flights of stairs, get "buzzed" into the locker room by Marge, who ran the front desk, and finally meet up with Lee, the swim instructor, who was standing in the shallow end of the pool. Lee was a great instructor who patiently dealt with a group of screaming boys whose adolescent voices echoed loudly off the pool walls like a subway train pulling into the station. We spent several Saturdays learning to bend our knees, hold our arms in a triangle over our heads and do a shallow dive into the pool. I graduated from Guppy to Minnow and, eventually, to Flying Fish and spent countless hours swimming around the pool practicing the basic swim strokes.

In the summer I swam in local lakes and ponds, including East Field, which was essentially a water-filled quarry with a beach. The water was so "suspect" that the city of Glens Falls added chlorine to it. It was strange to swim in a pond with chlorinated water. At ten years old my friends and I would ride our bikes to Round Pond and pay a penny a pound, which didn't amount to much more than a dollar, to jump off the pier into the murky waters of the pond to swim. When Round Pond closed its doors, we started riding our bikes to Gurney Lane in Queensbury. Gurney Lane was a cement pond, not a pool, treated with chlorine and surrounded by grassy hills and woods. I liked to go there as long as no one from my school saw me. Being that Gurney Lane had a playground, it wasn't considered a "cool place" to be hanging out.

As a teenager, I would ride my ten speed bike to Lake George and swim at Shepard's Park or the Million Dollar Beach which was much more "hip" than hanging out at Gurney Lane or East Field. One time my friend Bill and I got really ambitious and rode our bikes along dangerous Route 9 all the way to Bolton Landing to swim. Moreau Lake, Glen Lake, Haviland's Cove on the Hudson River and Lake George were our regular destinations since neither my friends nor I had swimming pools at our homes. I rode my bike everywhere.

One Sunday afternoon in early April of 1967, my grandfather, my dad and I took a ride to the Lake George Boat Company on Cleverdale Road on Harris Bay. There, in an old barn, was my grandfather's boat. The old wooden boat had been in storage for a few years and it was covered in dust and bird droppings and the rusty faded red boat trailer had two flat tires.

My grandfather had some health issues caused by several strokes and the boat just didn't get used. My dad made a deal with Mr. Thomas at the boat company regarding the outstanding storage fees, and a couple of weeks later the boat and its trailer showed up in our side yard on Kenworthy Avenue in Glens Falls. It soon became a destination for the neighborhood kids to play. My friends and I would climb into the boat and pretend to drive it, taking turns at the wheel. One day while hiding from my sister, Jackie, I climbed into the boat and hid under the front cabin underneath the steering wheel. While cramming my slender frame under the dashboard, I accidently knocked the steering cables off the wheel. Afraid that I would get punished, I frantically restrung the wire cables and forgot all about it.

Later that summer, when my dad got the 35 horsepower Evinrude outboard motor running, we towed the boat back up to Harris Bay, backed the trailer into the marina and pulled the boat over to an empty dock. I had secretly "paid off" my sister from going with us by promising her my favorite sticker book if she stayed home. My father was stumped as to why Jackie would not want to go to the lake for a boat ride, but I was jealous and didn't want her there with "the men." My dad and grandfather sat in the front seat of the boat and I sat by myself in the back seat, just the way I wanted it. My dad started up the motor, it sputtered out a bunch of gray oily smelling smoke which made me nervous but didn't seem to bother the older folks.

As we pulled out of the marina, my dad and my grandfather acted very "bothered" by something and I assumed it had to do with the motor. I could tell it was a serious discussion and they were trying to speak to each other over the noise of the sputtering outboard. The issue was that the steering column was wired backwards. When my dad turned the boat to the right, it turned left and when he turned it to the left, it went right. Apparently, when I "re-rigged" the cables at home in the yard I put them on upside down. I began to squirm as I saw large boats cruising down the lake towards us. I don't know if I was more afraid that we would get rammed by the other boats or that I would get in trouble for playing in the boat and messing up the cables. I wished my sister was there with me and I regretted having tricked her to stay home. I never did tell anyone that it was me that tangled the cables, but I did get in trouble when it was found out I bribed my sister to stay home.

My grandfather died in 1971 when I was in the fifth grade and that old wooden boat with the Evinrude outboard motor sat in my grandmother's back yard for several years covered with leaves and rotting away, never to be launched again. It was a sad reminder of happier days when my grandfather was in good health. He, his brother Cyrus and his wife, Rita, and my grandmother would cruise up the lake to Long Island for picnics. As for me and Jackie, we had more fun with the boat in our side yard than when it was on the lake.

My Aunt Judy was my first relative to own a fiberglass speed boat with an inboard engine as opposed to the Mercury and Evinrude outboards that my uncles dealt with. As she was a terrific water skier, the inboard engine helped provide a more powerful and consistent speed for Judy to ski behind. She kept it docked at Dunham's Bay for several years. Occasionally, I would go out with her on a waterskiing day. Judy was such an exceptional water skier that she was featured on a postcard of Lake George performing in a water ski pyramid. It was always intriguing to me to see that postcard in shops around Lake George knowing that my aunt was on top of that pyramid.

Uncle Mack got a deal on an old wooden boat that needed repairs, but it had an inboard motor as opposed to my grandfather's old outboard motorboat. Mack stated numerous times to me that he wouldn't own an outboard motor if someone gave him one for free. Mack's boat needed to be stripped down, sanded, and painted, which was a painstaking task. He kept his boat, covered with a tarp, in a field near Lake George. I would ride my bike up there and help him strip off the old paint, often in the hot sun with no shade. I would drink water from a thermos Mack brought while he would have a beer. Mack grew impatient with the stripping and sanding and finally said to me, "Let's just paint the damn thing." So, we did. We finished the boat by the end of the summer and in October we loaded up the boat with camping gear and headed up the lake to Long Island on an overnight boat trip. The inboard motor roared so loud that we couldn't hear any words that were spoken so we mostly communicated with hand signals, but the painted exterior and the stained dashboard looked great, like a classic wooden boat. Mack took a lot of pride in that boat.

Mack later managed the "Dock and Dine" restaurant in Hague, New York, on the northern end of Lake George. The restaurant had several docks adjacent to a stone walkway leading to the entrance. Hoping to attract folks from all over the lake, the owner was making a last-ditch effort to "make a go of it" by hiring Mack to manage the restaurant and bar. The concept was great, but for whatever reason, it was not a moneymaker. Mack's tenure at the Dock and Dine was just for a season, but one day while hanging out with him at the restaurant we decided to take the old wooden boat out for one of the grandest rides ever. We cruised along the northern most part of the lake to the old steamboat yard, into every hidden bay to check out the boathouses and then, full throttle on the blaring motor, we jetted across the lake, surely drawing the attention of anyone within miles. We felt like we belonged, officials of the Lake, fitting right in with this classic wooden boat.

Mack kept the boat for a few years and then, due to his ongoing financial "challenges," he sold it. It sat on a corner lot in the village of Lake George for several months before it sold. Every time I went by it, I thought of all the hard work we put into refurbishing it and that it deserved a better life than sitting on blocks on that corner.

My dad bought a used Rhodes 19 sailboat in the mid-Seventies and appropriately named it "Happy Days" after the television show. He kept the 19-foot-long boat moored near Assembly Point on Lake George. My dad knew enough about sailing so that we generally enjoyed our time on the boat, but us kids were always fearful of having no wind and just sitting there, together yet alone, in the middle of the lake. Thankfully, that never occurred. Many times we would just go to the Lake and swim out to the boat, hang out, then jump off the boat and swim back to the dock. To us kids, that was more fun than sailing.

When I was 18, my dad let me take the boat out with some of my friends. It was a beautiful sunny day with a steady breeze. My friends were impressed with my sailing ability and we were having a great time until my buddy's girlfriend fell over the side of the boat and into the lake. By the time we got the sails lowered, the outboard motor started, and the boat turned around we were hundreds of yards away from the drifting girl. We puttered up beside her as she floated in her life jacket and pulled her up into the boat right before we passed through a narrow section of the lake between Long Island and Assembly Point.

A year later, two of my college friends from Adirondack Community College, died in the exact same location. Dirk and Tom had been drinking, not wearing life jackets, and paddling a canoe to meet up with friends on Long Island when their canoe tipped over and they drowned, right in the middle of a sunny day.

Uncle Allan and Aunt Shirley had a nice wooden boat with an outboard motor from which I learned to water-ski.They were great teachers on how to water-ski and it wasn't long before they had me slalom skiing as I would get pulled up out of the water on two skis and then "drop" a ski. We would then circle around the lake looking for the lone ski. Their wooden boat survived the harshest of stress tests. We would load that boat with camping gear, boxes of food, firewood, fishing tackle, tire tubes and lots of kids, then Uncle Allan would drive it through a pouring rain, straining his eyes through the windshield to get us to a campsite on one of the islands. There were many times when I was sure the boat was going to bust open on a wave and send us crashing into Lake George. Uncle Allan made sure all the kids took a turn steering the boat. It didn't matter if we were pulling a skier, pulling up to a dock or driving at night, he wanted us to learn. I camped at the Narrows and the Mother Bunch Islands numerous times as a teenager and later with my oldest son, Jacob.

The weather on the islands was always windy and there was never a time when it didn't rain, but the most interesting part of camping on the islands was interacting with the people. On one camping trip we loaded up Uncle Allan's new fiberglass boat, with our camping gear and a kayak hanging off the back. Uncle Allan, Jacob (who was 10 at the time), and I headed up the lake to our campsite. When we arrived at the campsite it was occupied by another camper, even though we had the reservation. We were on our way to the Ranger station to report the situation when we spotted the Ranger cruising by in his patrol boat. Not realizing we were in a "no wake" zone, Uncle Allan sped off to catch up with the Ranger. The wake from our boat caused several cabin cruiser boats in the bay to rock violently back and forth. We waived down the Ranger and he told us to wait at a nearby campsite dock.

As we pulled up to the dock, two of the cabin cruiser owners, with heavy New York City accents, beer bellies and wife-beater tee shirts, pulled up beside us and started giving Uncle Allan a hard time, stating he had tipped over their cooking pots and caused damage to their boat cabins. One guy angrily stated, "My boat coulda caught on fire!" Jacob and I had been taking karate lessons together and the night before we left for Lake George, I had tested for my Green Belt and was all "jacked up" from doing 500 push-ups and sparring with other students. As I analyzed the current situation, I determined that if either one of these New York City thugs laid a hand on Uncle Allan, they were both going into the lake.

The boldest guy put his foot on our boat as a show of aggression and I started to strategize; a side kick to take out his knee and a front kick to the groin, perhaps a "shuto" strike to the neck and he was going down. Jacob sat in the boat nervously observing the situation. Uncle Allan pretended he didn't know it was a "no wake" zone and remained calm and collected, trying to be diplomatic. These guys weren't letting it go as they weren't going to answer to their angry wives who were watching from their dock that they did nothing. Just as the situation started escalating, the Ranger pulled up in his boat. The two enraged boaters then spewed out that they wanted to press charges against us for speeding in a no wake zone. They wanted a fight or a ticket. The Ranger looked at Uncle Allan, in his late sixties; Jacob, 10; and my 160-pound frame; and then looked at the two "Broad Street Bullies" and said, "Go back to your campsite, I will handle this." He didn't want to deal with them either. The two guys meandered back to their boat and left, loudly complaining about the local law's ineptness. The Ranger helped straighten out the campsite situation as well. As confident as I was in my karate skills, I was glad he showed up when he did.

Once we set up camp, we stayed out of that part of the lake, not wanting to tangle with those guys again. A favorite activity of mine was to go cliff diving (cannonball jumping) from various cliffs around the islands or on the eastern shore of the lake. We would pull up to cliffs in the boat, mooring 50 feet or so from the shore. Then we would swim to the shore, carefully climb up the cliffs to a height with which we were comfortable and jump away from the cliffs into the lake. There was always peer pressure to go higher on each jump.

Uncle Allan on Black Mountain summit

One year, when I was in my thirties, I witnessed what could have been a boating tragedy while camping on the islands with Uncle Allan, my son Jacob and Cousin Barbara. Allan had picked up Walt Brennan at the dock in Bolton Landing and brought him and his grandchildren out to our campsite for the day. About 30 feet from shore was a flat rock that was 10" under the surface of the water. I would lay flat on my back on the rock with my face just out of the water. There were warning buoys around the rock to prevent anyone from driving over it. The younger kids would stand on the rock, ankle-deep in water, and jump into the lake.

Later that evening, just as we sat down for dinner, we observed an outboard motorboat loaded with loud, screaming people on a joyride around the lake, speeding around the islands. It caught our attention because the folks were so loud, trying to talk over the roar of their outboard motor. Right before our eyes the boat sped past the warning buoys and skimmed over the flat rock. We heard the grinding of the metal boat and the roar of the outboard motor as the lower unit slammed against the rock and kicked up out of the water. It sounded like a car collision. They were going so fast that the boat made a few slow circles as it floated out into the middle of the lake. We ran to the shoreline and yelled out: "Do you need help?" We got a chorus of "No" from the crew in heavy New York City accent.

Evidently some kids from the city had rented a boat from the marina in Bolton Landing and were not familiar with how the buoy system worked in the lake. As we stood on the shore contemplating what we could do to help them, another camper wandered up, curiously observing the situation. When he suggested that we go out and help them, Walt said sarcastically: "I think they are from New York City" to which our neighboring camper, also with a heavy New York City accent, said: "Yeah, what of it? I'm from the city. Is there something wrong with that?" Walt, knowing who he was dealing with, quickly covered his tracks by saying: "Oh, they just might not be familiar with the lake."

That reply seemed to appease the onlooker. The crew in the boat, finally realizing their predicament, starting yelling "Help! Help!" Before we could get out to them, a Lake George patrol boat showed up and towed them to shore. Once the group was safely on shore, we went over to look at the boat. The motor was torn off the transom and the bottom of the boat had huge scrape marks throughout. There was a foot of water lining the bottom of the boat. Fortunately, none of the group was injured but the boat was totaled. The next day the same group of kids were back out on the lake, speeding around the islands in a newly rented boat from the marina.

In 1999, to celebrate our wedding, my wife, Terri, and I decided to take our newly blended family to Lake George. We climbed Buck Mountain, played putt-putt golf and did the usual tourist things in the village. Uncle Allan took us out tubing on the lake.

Noelle, our oldest daughter at 15, was not a fan of climbing Buck Mountain, having complained during the entire hike. She took her revenge on me by driving the boat while I was being pulled on the tube. What could be more enticing than having your new stepdad go flying off a tube into the lake with everyone watching? Never a big fan of tubing myself, I reluctantly agreed to go. Of course, the gig was for the kids to encourage Noelle to "dump me." When I climbed back into the boat my wedding ring, of three days, was gone, having slipped off my finger while holding on to the tow rope. How fitting for all my years of swimming and boating in Lake George to have my wedding ring sink to the bottom of the lake. Terri was not very happy about it, saying, "Well, you didn't have *that* very long."

In a twist of fate, on our 10th wedding anniversary we went to Schroon Lake and, while on a canoe trip down the Schroon river, Terri lost her wedding ring. I guess if you are going to lose something as significant as a wedding ring, what could be more romantic than having it slowly sink to the bottom of an Adirondack waterway?

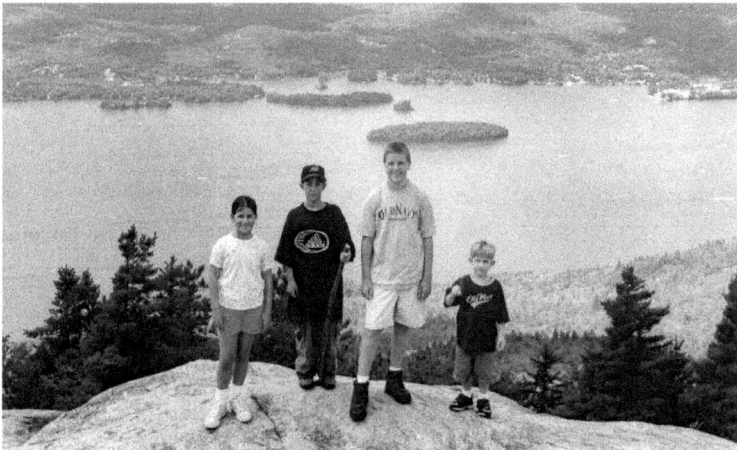

Danielle, Ryan, Jacob & Shane on top of Buck Mountain, 1999

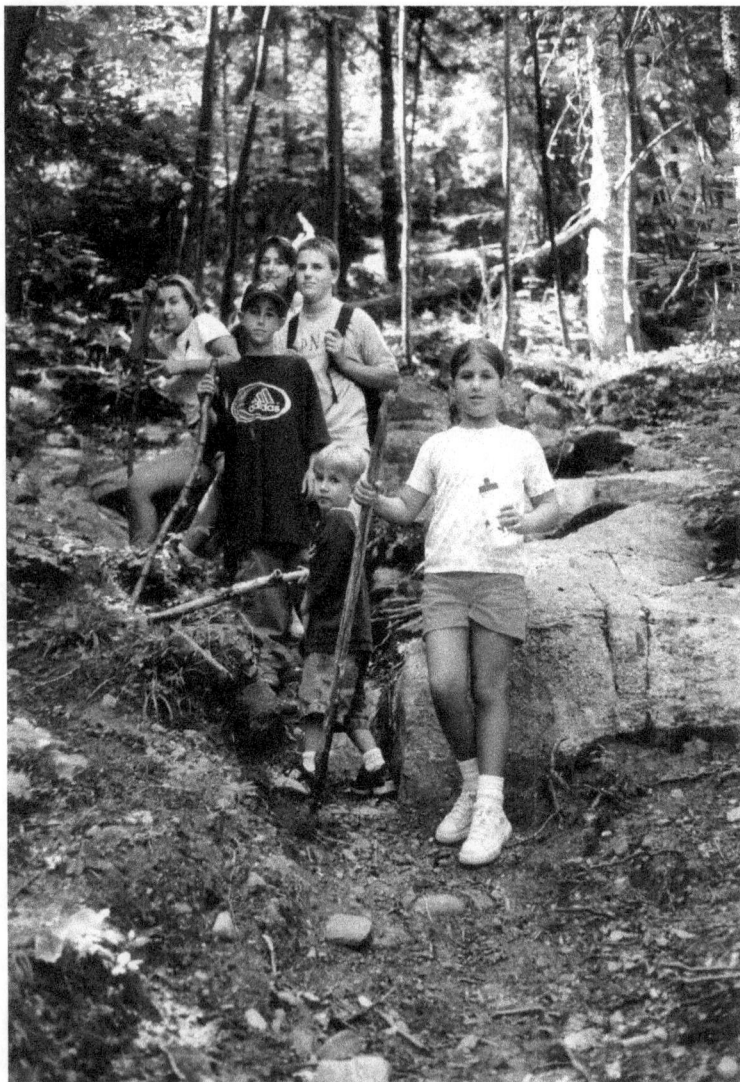

First hike with the new family group, Buck Mountain, 1999

Laundromats

There was a saying in our family that when the local farmers needed rain for their crops, they would call anyone with the last name of Dean and encourage them to go camping. I can count on one hand the times that I have camped in the Adirondacks and it did not rain. It may have rained only for a few hours or it may have rained for a few days, but it rained. In my later years of tent camping, I conceded victory to the rain and purchased a car port and a giant tarp to set up over our tent at the campground. It worked out well for keeping the tent dry, but it looked out of place on the campsite. As folks walked by I'm sure they were thinking there was either a vehicle under the tarp or I was just making the prestigious Adirondack campground look trashy. No one ever complimented me on the idea, but no one ever told me to remove it either. It was a final solution to years of pent-up frustration of leaking tents, wet sleeping bags and drips of rainwater creeping their way across the tent and onto my pillow. Sure, the poles were heavy, and it took a good half hour to put it all together, but it was worth it— no more dreaded trips to the local laundromat.

We always had a washer and dryer at home, so we never went to a laundromat in Glens Falls. However, once we started tent camping, Adirondack laundromats became well-known to us. The first laundromat I ever visited was in Ticonderoga in the mid-Sixties. I'm not sure when or where laundromats started showing up in the Adirondack Park, but the Ticonderoga laundromat has to be in contention as one of the originals. The Ticonderoga laundromat is on a corner right off the main street in the downtown area. I first went there with my Aunt Ginny and cousins Jeff and Karen on "laundry day." It was interesting at first as we checked out the washing machines and the glass-door dryers. As a youngster of seven years old, I was easily entertained by watching the colorful clothes go round and round. The sounds were entertaining as well—the humming of the washing machines, the accidental slamming of the machine lids and the chitchat of the older women tending to their clothes. It made the time pass by quickly.

The first "laundry day" was interesting, but by the third and fourth "laundry day" the event became a chore. When we started camping at Putts Pond, we always included a trip to the Ticonderoga laundromat as part of our week of camping. Five kids with wet, muddy clothes and toddlers with cloth diapers were a sure recipe for a trip to the laundromat. Even as an unobservant kid, I would recognize the same women doing their weekly laundry and the "caretaker" woman who organized the magazines and closed the dryer doors proclaiming, "This washer works over here," as several washers did not work. We didn't even live in Ticonderoga, yet I was recognizing the "locals" at the laundromat.

Thirty years later, in the 1990s, I was camping at Putts Pond with my oldest son, Jacob, when we got poured upon and naturally our sleeping bags got wet. We made the 20-minute trek into Ticonderoga and to my surprise the same laundromat, on the same corner, was still in business. We entered through the side door and I instantly had a deja vu moment. The washing machines and dryers and even the magazines were exactly as I remembered them in the 1960s and some of the machines even had hand-written "out of order" signs taped on their metal lids. An older woman was tending to the machines and sweeping the floor; for all I knew, she was the same woman who was doing that 30 years prior. We put our wet sleeping bags into the dryers and wandered down the street to purchase night crawlers for fishing. I realized I was now passing the "laundromat visitation ritual" to the next generation of Dean campers.

Another frequently-visited laundromat was the Long Lake village laundry. Long and narrow, it was difficult to "hang out" in that laundromat and, based upon the number of sleeping bags churning in the dryers, it was always crowded with other rain-soaked campers. Once we started camping at Lake Eaton, the Long Lake laundromat was entered into our camp itinerary. One year we broke tradition and camped at the Harris Lake campground in Newcomb. Apparently, Newcomb didn't have a laundromat because after it rained and our clothes and sleeping bags got wet, we headed to the Long Lake laundromat with our activity books in hand to occupy our time.

Twenty years later I was camping at Lake Eaton with my sister, Jackie, and our boys whom we decided to let chose our campsite. Jared and Jacob chose the only site that was below sea level. It was dry when we set up the tents and dining canopy, but when it rained the entire campsite was under water. Jackie and her two boys packed up and hit the road, leaving Jacob and myself scratching our heads as to what to do. The picnic table was in ankle-deep water and our remaining tent was sagging and surrounded by mud. As expected, we bundled up our wet sleeping bags, threw them into the back of the car and headed to the Long Lake laundromat. We stuck it out one more night before packing up all our wet belongings and heading home.

That wasn't the last time that we packed up at Lake Eaton. A year later we were camping on higher ground, but after three days of rain we just threw everything, soaking wet though it was, into the back of the station wagon and headed home. Once we got home, the gear sat in the back of the car for several days until I got motivated enough to set it all up to dry out.

Ten years later, in 2003, we had another similar incident at Lake Eaton with our tents and sleeping bags getting soaked. I've come to believe that Lake Eaton is the epicenter for Adirondack rainstorms.

In 2004, I took a few of the boys to Lake Durant for a camping trip. It was cloudy and misty when we set up camp, but we had high hopes for a fun trip. The next morning, we set out early to climb Cascade Mountain. While on the hike it started to rain. Little did we know how much it had rained back at Lake Durant. When we got back to our campsite, the tent was collapsing from the weight of the water and the contents of our tent were soaked. We quickly loaded the wet bags and clothes into the car and headed to Long Lake to the laundromat where we loaded our gear into several dryers. While we waited for our items to dry, we picked up some snacks at the corner market.

It rained all night and by morning everything was wet again. I surrendered to the rain once again and told the boys we were packing up and heading home. They were upset and tried to convince me to take them back to the laundromat in Long Lake. "I'm sick of laundromats," I proclaimed. "I'll take you to McDonalds in Old Forge on the way home."

In 2009, we purchased a camp near Parishville that has running water and a metal roof so I thought my laundromat days were over. I was wrong. Wet towels, muddy shorts and dirty sheets can't make it through a full week of Adirondack weather. Now the nearby Potsdam laundromat is our new best friend. Four to five times every summer my wife and I go on a laundromat date to Potsdam. We tried the South Colton laundromat but that was too "rustic" for our simple ways. The Potsdam laundromat has a thrift store next door which easily allows time for the clothes to go through an extra cycle in the dryer. One of the criteria for Adirondack laundromats must be that the caretaker be an older woman with gray hair, glasses and wearing an outdated dress because there is no way there can be only one of them when the woman in Potsdam in 2019 looks just like the woman in Ticonderoga in 1967.

As long as there is rain in the Adirondacks, there will be a calling for laundromats.

Santanoni

My wife Terri's exact words were: "I am never doing this again!" She was referring not only to the attempt at climbing Santanoni Mountain, but also to the entire idea of a family camping trip. We sat in the dimly-it car recapping the day's events, using the car as a soundproof booth in the middle of the Harris Lake campground. As our kids sat around the crackling campfire poking sticks into the flames, their contented countenances reflected that they had moved on from the pitiful events of the day. Other campers were settled down in their campsites and you could hear the loons cooing on the lake and the bullfrogs' "brivetts" as darkness enveloped the campground. Outside of our car, it was peaceful. Inside of our car sat two physically and emotionally exhausted parents who needed to shield themselves from the families who had actually had a nice day.

As a family, we had done small hikes up Blue Mountain and Buck Mountain, but we had never camped together and had certainly never attempted climbing a high peak, a classification for a mountain over 4,000 feet. But I was a dreamer. Wouldn't it be great to take four of our children, a teenage niece and Terri on a camping trip and climb a high peak? After years of hiking with my buddies, my expectation was that the experience would only get better if we did it as a family. I had expectations of the laughs, the exercise and the bonding that would surely take place.

I assured Terri that we could pull it off. I had personally hiked many of the high peaks starting at a young age and I savored the memories. My parents took our family camping every summer so there couldn't be that much that could go wrong. Terri, knowing the kid's personalities better than I, was a bit skeptical about the idea, but shared in my high expectations.

The plan was to leave our campsite at Harris Lake by 9:00 a.m., drive 30 minutes to the parking area at the old Tahawus iron mines, walk the road to the trailhead of Santanoni Mountain and start climbing. Santanoni Mountain was close by and offered gorgeous views of Newcomb and the Long Lake area where we were camping. Not being totally convinced the kids were all on board with climbing a high peak, I ran the idea past Terri one more time as a safety net, as if to say it was "our idea" rather than "my idea." Terri threw the ball right back in my court. "I trust you," is all she said. What she meant was: "I'm not dealing with any complaining kids."

Of course, I conveniently left out some of the details of the hike, such as Santanoni is a "trail less" peak. This meant the trail is not maintained by the State and it is recommended the person leading the hike be experienced in using a compass and a map and be well-versed in encouraging disgruntled hikers. Well, I *did* have a topographical map and surely, with all the folks trudging up and down that mountain, the trail would be well-worn.

Our lunches were made, our water bottles full and our assortment of back packs loaded in the car. It was a warm and slightly humid summer day. After re-convincing everyone that this was going to be a great time, we loaded up the van, intent on keeping with our plan, which would get us back to our campsite by dinner.

At 4,607 feet, Santanoni Mountain is the 14th highest mountain in New York State. When I mentioned that fact to the kids before we started hiking, they were intrigued, but did not understand what that meant in physical effort. (When I mentioned that fact after the hike, I received some colorful responses that normally would have resulted in punishment but somehow seemed appropriate, even to a parent.) The trail head sign said 4.4 miles to the lean-to and then a shorter distance to the summit. A 4-mile hike on a sunny summer day didn't sound so bad; in fact, everyone started out in a chipper mood. The girls were giggling about their outfits and the boys bragging about their skateboarding stunts.

After a very short distance we hit our first speed bump. Terri needed to go to the bathroom. I was politely asked: "Where do I go?"

"Hmmm," I replied, "Do you prefer a pine tree or an oak tree?"

Apparently my carefully laid out plans left out the information about "bathroom breaks" of which I may have underestimated the importance. Following some humbling efforts on Terri's part, we moved onward.

After a couple of miles of mostly flat hiking through low brush and meadows, we crossed paths with a group of hikers coming down the mountain. I was a little offended as they stood and gawked, scoping out my family. As they observed Shane and Ryan's skateboarding sneakers, Danielle's "Dora the Explorer" back pack along with her designer brand shorts, Jacob dressed in camo gear and Terri with her sweater wrapped around her waist, they most likely thought: "Don't they know this is a high peak and not some nature walk?"

The youngest child at age seven, Shane, liked to lead the group since he had the most energy and his skateboarding sneakers were already covered in the black muck that shadowed the sides of the trail. The muck drew an array of comments from our family such as: "Whoa Shane, that's rich!" and

"I'm sure that will wash off" to "Those were brand new sneakers!" I won't say who said what.

As the trail began to ascend steeply up the mountain and we
began to grab onto roots and rocks, our attitudes began to
descend. Water and snack breaks came more frequently. The
breaks were so frequent that I commented that we really needed
to pick up the pace and that we needed to conserve some of the
snacks and water for later. Those comments were not well-
received, and, in the unofficial report card of the hike planner, it
went down as "strike one." I was reminded by Terri that this was
a family hike and I was not addressing the workers at my job.

The two older kids, Jacob and Morgan, thought it would
be "more fun" if they went ahead of the group and scouted out
the trail. That worked fine for a short time until we somehow
lost track of them. We all began to yell out to them, even using
a whistle to attract them. They eventually re-joined the rest of
the group, but not before generating a little more stress and
adding an hour to the hike.

At 1:00 p.m. we reached the lean-to, stopped for lunch and
wondered how much further it was to the top, being disheart-
ened that the 4.4 miles did not bring us to that lofty spot. The
hot mid-day sun, combined with the steep climb, made for
some major bickering among the group and conjured up comments like: "We could be at the beach right now," and "We
could be skateboarding right now," and "We could be doing
just about anything but this right now." I pretended I did not
hear the "Whose idea was this?" comment. At around 4:00
p.m. we hit a patch of blown-down trees. As we started weav-
ing our way over and under the downed trees, we came to the
realization that this may not even be the trail.

Fortunately, three athletic-looking guys with professional
hiking gear, looking like they just stepped out of an outdoor
apparel catalog, came briskly hiking down the mountain, bare-

ly breaking a sweat. With an apparent mission on tap, they did not stop to chat, but I was able to get out of them that the top of the mountain was "only 20 minutes away." That is, twenty minutes by their standard. It was time for a family huddle with anyone that was still talking to me. Everyone agreed that 20 minutes to that group of professional hikers meant at least an hour hike to our exhausted crew of amateurs. That was all we agreed about. The two oldest voted to go to the top because, "How could we go this far and not make the extra effort?" The rest of the kids were done. There was no vote. They didn't even have to be asked. They were over this hiking thing and wanted to go back to camp. Terri did the math and estimated that darkness would fall in a few hours and wisely decided the last place "we" wanted to be was on a mountain in the dark. Terri used her "super delegate" vote to "go back to camp." I wisely abstained from voting.

And so, there we sat, having hiked over five miles in the last seven hours, sitting among blown-down trees in the 80-degree hot sun, dirt and muck forming streaks on our sweaty faces. With the pink backpacks and the bling on the girl's shirts and designer shorts, we could have passed for a group from a rock music festival. Maybe Dora the Explorer would have been proud of us, but no one in our defeated group had any words of encouragement. The mountain had won. We took our last bites of any remaining snacks, finished off the last drops of our water and began our solemn retreat down the mountain. It seemed like a march towards a prison camp with me in the rear of the group and no one bothering to look back to see how far behind I was or even if I was still around. The consensus might have been that, hopefully, I had fallen so far behind that I had gotten lost.

As we reached the old mining road that led to the parking lot, the sun was no longer beating down on us. The sun's rays darted in and out of the trees forming long shadows on the dirt road. I ran several scenarios through my mind, being afraid to speak out load, about how we could have made it to the top and still gotten back to the car by dark. I finally conceded to myself that it just wasn't meant to be. The kids began talking to each other again, but not to me. Some smiles occurred, but probably only because the van was in sight. Terri was right. It most likely would have been dark on the hike down the mountain if we had continued on to the top; and it would also have been catastrophic since we had not prepared to hike at night and did not bring flashlights. Moans of "I'm hungry!" and "What's for dinner?" and "What time is it anyway?" dominated the ride back to the campground. The dream of camping and hiking with my family had turned out to be a bad idea, and . . . I was to blame.

Trying to salvage the family camping trip, the next day we ventured to the Long Lake beach. The trampoline and diving board on the town raft were therapeutic for our withered group as the kids were once again in their realm of expertise, swimming and diving. As Terri and I sat on the town beach working through the "what went wrongs" of the camping trip, the three boys interrupted and pleaded to go on a seaplane ride. I assured them that it was way too costly to take seven people on a seaplane ride. Our oldest son, Jacob, implied that the man who operated the plane would give us a deal. At that point, I was willing to do anything to redeem myself. Seeing the opportunity to restore my credibility, I wandered down to the beach and asked Mr. Helms what the "deal" was. The entire family was glaring at me as I inquired about the flying. I knew by their piercing looks that any answer other than "we're going" was going to rekindle yesterday's debacle. Either by divine intervention or because he somehow sensed my predicament and felt pity for me, Mr. Helms said: "Fifty dollars but the smallest one will have to sit on a lap."

It was a chance at redemption. As we loaded into the seaplane, the boys started talking to me again and as the plane climbed over the 4,000-foot plateau, the pilot, unaware of our prior day's failed adventure, pointed out "to the right is the top of Santanoni Mountain."

Ah yes, there it was, the bald rocks through the clearing of the trees. We did make it to the top, via the use of a seaplane. The pain of the previous day and the "I'm never doing that again!" were quickly forgiven.

Baby Diver

When my father decided he wouldn't be using his 8-foot wooden bed utility trailer anymore, it was passed on to my family. Pulled behind our mini-van, we mostly used it for hauling construction scraps to the dump, moving our daughter Danielle to numerous apartments each time a lease expired, and for family camping trips. For the camping trips, we would load up the trailer with all our tents, lawn chairs—anything that could tolerate getting wet—and then tie our two canoes on top to hold everything in place.

As I was strapping down the canoes for a trip to Eighth Lake my wife, Terri, peeked out at the driveway from the garage, wondering when "we" would be ready to go—"We" being Shane, our 12-year-old son; Trevor, Shane's friend; myself; and our 2½ year old son, Ashton. Terri was sitting this trip out (as usual) and her casual observation of loading the trailer was in gleeful anticipation of having the house to herself for a week and being relieved that she didn't have to spend that week sleeping in a tent with a two-year-old.

Ashton had a lot of energy as a toddler, more than any of our other children, and we were continually challenged to find ways for him to burn off his excess energy. There is a park behind our home and either Terri or I would take him there to use the swing set—for hours at a time—or just to run around the baseball diamond until he was (or we were) tired out.

One of Ashton's favorite activities as a baby was to take

baths—two-hour long baths with a tub full of toys. It is not unusual for a baby to enjoy a warm bath but what *was* unusual was that he loved to hold his breath, put his face under the bath water and look for toys laying on the bottom of the tub.

In November 2005, when Ashton turned two years old, I started taking him to the downtown Syracuse YMCA pool to teach him to swim. Ashton instantly took to the warm water as if it were a giant bathtub and he was jumping off the side into the pool and my waiting arms on our first visit. Although he wasn't performing any formal swim strokes, he did have a unique ability to hold his breath and maneuver under water without any fear of opening his eyes. Soon he was working his way to the bottom of the shallow end of the pool looking for his toys that I had tossed a few feet away. The YMCA lifeguard was initially very concerned about what was going on and nervously watched Ashton like a hawk, expecting to have to fly in and rescue him at any time.

After several weeks of observing and getting to know us, the lifeguard would watch in amazement as Ashton dived to the bottom of the pool to retrieve his toys. Also, I tried to teach Ashton basic swim strokes, but his mindset was to hold his breath, kick his legs and swim to the bottom. Since even the shallow end was over his head, he was dependent upon holding on to the side of the pool until he learned to tread water. It was a great way to get out his excess energy, even if it meant I had to get into the pool as well; but we anxiously waited for the summer weather so we could escape going to the downtown Syracuse Y to swim.

Once we arrived at Eighth Lake and set up our campsite, we did our usual exploring of the area and then headed to the beach. It soon became apparent that the beach at Eighth Lake was not appealing to the two 12-year-old boys; in fact, they used the term "lame" to describe it. Although the Eighth Lake beach is a nice family beach, Shane and Trevor weren't interested in "family time." I told them I would take them to the best beach in the Adirondacks on the next sunny day. Two days later the four of us trekked northward to the Long Lake Town Beach. Shane had vaguely recalled going there a few years earlier on our Santanoni Mountain trip, but when he saw the seaplanes parked on the side of the beach he perked right up and was telling Trevor about his prior flight in the blue seaplane.

Once we parked the car and got situated on the beach, Shane asked me about taking another seaplane ride. Recalling how the pilot of the plane, Mr. Helms, gave our family such a great deal three years prior, I decided to see if he was working that day. Much to Shane and Trevor's delight, Mr. Helms was working that day and gave us another deal we could not refuse. Ashton could sit on my lap and he would only charge us for three—good enough for me, as I was trying to gain credibility with the teenagers. Shane sat in front with Mr. Helms and was very inquisitive about the operation of the seaplane. Ashton sat quietly on my lap while Trevor looked out the window at the kids jumping off the raft. We taxied up the lake, took off and casually climbed to a suitable flying altitude. I was enjoying the scenery, in awe of the giant shadows that the clouds had blanketed over the mountains, when the plane suddenly took a nosedive straight for Long Lake.

We dropped several hundred feet in a matter of seconds. I sat there holding Ashton tight while Trevor clutched the sides of his seat. In the front seats Mr. Helms and Shane were calm and collected. When they heard me gasping, Mr. Helms chuckled and said to Shane, "I guess we should have warned them of what we were about to do." Apparently, Shane had asked Mr. Helms about the diving capabilities of his seaplane. Ashton had fallen asleep on my lap and was oblivious to any of the flight happenings and Trevor was grinning as he replied,

"That was cool."

After a smooth landing, we taxied up to the dock. Ashton woke up and asked about joining the other kids he saw jumping off the raft. The teenage boys immediately jumped off the end of the dock and swam towards the raft with the rope swing and mini trampoline. Ashton wanted to join them, no doubt thinking about how he had jumped into the pool at the YMCA. After I explained the dangers of jumping into the deep water and the difference between the Y and the lake, he was good with hanging out with me on the beach. I grabbed a small shiny rock from near the dock and tossed it into the shallow area where we were swimming. It sunk to the sandy bottom a few feet below. Ashton took a deep breath and worked his way under the water until he spotted the rock and proudly held it up as he resurfaced from the lake. I then tossed the rock a few feet further away and once again he took a deep breath, scoured the lake floor until he found the rock and then bopped to the surface. To make it more challenging, the two of us wandered over to the non-swimming area and found a few more shiny stones.

We went back to the beach area and I tossed four shiny rocks into the lake. Ashton took a deep breath and grabbed two of the rocks before coming up for a breath and going back underwater. Within 20 seconds, Ashton was proudly holding four shiny stones, two in each little hand. As we continued this routine, we didn't notice the line of people standing on the shoreline watching us. It wasn't until another child had a temper tantrum that we became aware of the spectators. The parents were scolding their son because he was afraid to go into the water. The parents, in an attempt to encourage their child to get wet, shouted out across the beach, "How old is your son that is diving for rocks?" When I stated that he was two years old the father said to his son, "You're five years old! Look at that two-year-old dive for rocks!"

I was a little embarrassed for saying Ashton was only two. Ashton's only reply was, "Throw the rocks again, Dad." I said, "Why don't we take a break and go get an ice cream." It was never our intent to have an audience to our father-and-son diving routine.

We tried the Eighth Lake beach again before breaking camp and heading home, but everyone quickly became bored and thought that surely I had a better idea that was more entertaining. The shallow end was too shallow to dive for rocks and the deep end had no dock to jump off and no raft with a mini trampoline. There were no seaplanes, no ice cream stands, no shiny stones, no motorcycles humming past the beach, just a serene Adirondack lake. It may have been "lame" to a teenager, but it was much sought-after tranquility for the one who had to pack the car and load up the trailer.

Baby Diver in action

Prospect Mountain

Nursing homes are dream killers. Folks who reside in them often finish out their lives living without hope in a discouraging environment, their dreams reduced to a mealtime gathering or a monthly visit from a caring but time-challenged relative. My dad, Jerry, who resided in a nursing home for five years, was an exception. He never stopped dreaming. Even up to the week he died he dreamed of planting his garden once again. He dreamed of moving into the old brick country farmhouse that he had lived in as a child. He dreamed of once again hiking in the Adirondacks. "Not the high peaks, of course," he would say, but some of "the lesser ones" that he knew like the back of his hand. After all, he grew up in the area and when he wasn't hiking or boating, he was searching maps and reading trail books for his next Adirondack excursion.

As the oldest son in the family, I was privileged to be doing more activities with my dad than my other siblings. Many of those activities revolved around lakes, mountains and ballparks. My first hike with my dad was Prospect Mountain on Lake George. It was early June in 1968 and, since we lived only 20 minutes away, we had the luxury of what my father would say was "waiting out the weather," which simply meant we weren't hiking in the rain. We hiked the two-mile trail that day in shorts and tee-shirts. My dad really wanted it to be an enjoyable experience for me; my sister, Jackie; and my friend, Tim, who were also on their first mountain climb. We filled our metal army surplus canteens with fresh water and packed lots of homemade trail mix which my dad called "gorp." We used my dad's "gorp" recipe for years to come—raisins, peanuts, Cheerios and chocolate chips.

According to my dad, who was a biology teacher, each ingredient played an essential role in maintaining the stamina needed for hiking. My dad made sure he was building a foundation of the basics for us to use on future hikes, of which there would be many. As we hiked up Prospect Mountain, the peacefulness of the breeze brushing gently over the treetops was rudely interrupted by a noisy road crew constructing a new road. The road would eventually run five miles from Lake George Village to the top of the mountain. The sunburned road crew workers in yellow hard hats and muscle shirts were yelling to each other over the roar of the bulldozer engine. The sound of metal scraping off a rock echoed around the trees as a large road grader made its way past us. Tim and I were intrigued by the heavy equipment, too young to understand the "forever wild" way of thinking that my dad embraced. In fact, it added a new dimension to the hike, much to my father's dismay. The entire scene of building the road brought several comments from my dad, like: "Why do they have to go and build a road?" and "This used to be a great mountain to hike." Progress was not often looked upon favorably by my dad. In fact, he boycotted the local mall for several years. His reason was, "It's ruining the downtown business," which he repeated countless times in our home.

After leaving the construction crew behind us and reaching the mountain summit, it was peaceful again as the top was still undeveloped. We turned and looked back at where we had started from just below the Northway and, fortunately, the road work was out of sight from our viewpoint. We gazed upon Lake George and the surrounding area as my dad pointed out familiar landmarks, like the Hudson River, to us kids. We ate our sandwiches and raisins near the rusty metal cable wheel that was all that remained of an old railway that had led to a hotel on the mountaintop. We curiously scoured the grounds looking for artifacts that the Iroquois Indians may have left behind. Being on top of Prospect Mountain exceeded our expectations of what it would be like.

As we crossed the freshly graded dirt road and the construction crew on the way back down the mountain, my dad frowned. He could have said more words of disgust that I'm sure were in his thoughts, but he chose not to say anything. We knew. The point had already been made.

The sun was shining, there was a slight breeze and it was early June. It was 45 years after our first hike up Prospect Mountain and I was pulling my dad, strapped to his wheelchair, into the van. He had been paralyzed since suffering a stroke. The two of us were going back up Prospect Mountain. I stopped at the toll booth to pay the 10-dollar fee to use the road up the mountain. There was a time when my dad would have commented on the fee, but not today, not in this season of his life.

Driving up the mountain I thought about dad's disapproval of building the road, but fonder memories quickly took over. It was a quiet ride up the mountain. Since dad had suffered the stroke, he wasn't up on current events and most of our conversations only required short answers about my job or the weather.

Oddly, we did not encounter any other cars on the ride up the mountain and there was only one other family at the top, and they left shortly after we arrived. We had the top of Prospect Mountain to ourselves, just like it was on our first hike.

In the early years of the 20th Century, Prospect Mountain was home to the Prospect Mountain House which entertained those willing to take the cable car to the top of the mountain. The House burned to the ground about a hundred years ago but rusty iron gears and cables protruding out of the ground act as reminders of the past glory of the mountain.

My dad and I sat on a flat rocky point at the edge of the summit and looked at the dark blue water of Lake George looming below us. My dad once had a sailboat on Lake George —that was another dream he had and one that he lived out in his life. I wheeled him to a spot next to the rusty iron cable wheel, most likely the same spot where we had sat 45 years earlier. The rocks and rusty cables had not changed. Only my dad and I had changed. We sat there for 30 minutes picking places out of the landscape that we had visited over the years. There was Assembly Point, where he kept his sailboat moored. There was Buck Mountain, where we picked blueberries. There was Fort George, where we often picnicked and, to the far right, was the city of Glens Falls, where we both were raised and graduated from the same high school.

I said "Dad, do you remember our first hike up this mountain?" As I leaned in closer to him, he softly spoke something about "building the road." This time there was no frown or grumbling of protest about progress, only reflection. The road of progress had enabled my dad and I to fulfill a dream and climb Prospect Mountain together one last time.

First mountain climb, Prospect Mountain, 1968. Left to right: Tim Brennan, the author and his sister Jackie.

Construction of the Prospect Mountain Highway

Last "climb" of Prospect Mountain with my father

One Last Adventure

In an effort to save a few bucks, we had recently purchased a kayak from the Potsdam Walmart. By buying the kayak on-line and picking it up in Potsdam on the way to our camp, we could save 40 dollars. Potsdam is only 30 miles from camp as opposed to the 180-mile trip from Syracuse. I was confident we could just tie the kayak on top of Terri's Nissan Rogue for the short trip from Potsdam. The Walmart store manager assisted me in carrying the kayak from the sporting goods section of the store out to the sidewalk where Terri and our two dogs were waiting in the car. Seeing the kayak laying on the concrete sidewalk next to the car, it appeared to me that it would fit inside. Why bother with all the rope when it could just slide inside?

Terri helped me unload some items out of the back of the car and held the dogs by their leashes while I positioned the kayak into the car. At a slight angle with the front seat folded down, it fit "snuggly," but looked to me like it would work out fine. Terri wasn't so sure. She calmly inquired if it was "going to work that way." I assured her it was fine and slammed down the trunk door to make sure it clicked tight. Just as I heard the click of the trunk, I saw the nose of the kayak break through the windshield. Since it was shatterproof glass, Terri didn't hear the break but saw the blood drain out of my face. "Is everything alright?" she asked. "Take a look at the windshield!" I replied. We both looked at each other without expression and in disbelief as we saw the plastic green kayak that had poked through the broken glass.

After making numerous phone calls to windshield replacement shops throughout the North Country, from Ogdensburg to Plattsburgh, it was determined that we could not get a new windshield until well into the next week. We cautiously drove to camp hoping the remainder of the windshield would hold up. Once we arrived at camp our neighbor, a local woodsman—a jack-of-all-trades type of guy—calmly said: "That can be fixed with duct tape."

As he went about duct taping our windshield, I wondered how the wipers would work if it rained. There was no way we were driving back to Syracuse if it rained. Fortunately, two days later we had a perfect sunny summer day and we drove home with half a windshield—all to save $40!

Author on top of Phelps Mountain, 1974

Conclusion

There is a certain tranquility that one can experience by hiking or kayaking alone. The "one-with-nature" feeling that allows you to stop when you want, go where you want and make whatever proclamations you feel led to bring forth. One morning recently when I was at our camp, I got up just as it was getting light, yet before the sun came up. I paddled my kayak alone across the glass-still lake to the opposite shoreline, which was mostly primitive forestland. As I approached a marshy area between eroded tree stumps poking up out of the flat water, I noticed a deer slowly turning its head to get a better glimpse at me. After the deer's curiosity was satisfied, it bolted over the marshy brush and disappeared into the woods.

As I paddled up the lake, the mist hovering all around me slowly began to dissipate as the sunlight crept over the tree-tops. Off to my right I heard a rustling in the woods and pulled the blade of my paddle out of the water and let it rest on the kayak. As I sat 10 yards from shore, being as quiet as I could be, a well-fed muscular coyote emerged from the dark of the woods. The coyote stayed right on course as if following its morning routine only to stop, sniff around and identify the odd smell of a human being, then continued its jaunt along the shoreline before heading back into a dense hemlock patch.

As I paddled further up the lake, the sun crept up over the horizon and planted itself firmly into the sky, burning off the remaining haze. I stopped paddling when I noticed a bald eagle circling overhead. It wasn't as uncommon to see a bald eagle from a kayak as it was the coyote, but it was a nice con-clusion to the morning paddle.

On the way back to camp I realized it was comforting to be so close to nature, but it would have been even nicer to have had other people with me to share in the adventure. I have rarely hiked, paddled, camped, or skied alone for that very rea-son. It is one thing to share your experiences with others, like I have with this book, yet the adventures would be meaningless without people there to either contribute to the event or be witnesses of it.

I have concluded that the majesty and mysticism of the Adirondack Park has only slightly influenced my life. It is more the people, with their own experiences and personalities, who have encouraged and engaged with me in the Adirondacks: They have impacted my life the most. Hiking with a large group from an outing club doesn't sound appealing to me, but it does hold the potential to create some rainy-day musings.